LANCE

LANCE

A Testament of Grace

Dave Breese

Awana Clubs International
3201 Tollview Drive • Rolling Meadows, Illinois 60008

131127

AWANA CLUBS INTERNATIONAL
3201 Tollview Drive
Rolling Meadows, IL 60008

Awana Clubs International
is a worldwide Bible-centered
youth organization. The
primary aim of Awana is to
reach boys and girls with the
gospel of Jesus Christ and then
train them to serve Him.

Printed in the United States of America

Webster tells us that a lance is a weapon of war. This book is about a "Lance" — a man who has been a tool in the hand of God, used mightily in the warfare against principalities and powers — a Lance for the Lord.

Contents

Contents

Preface

Who could have predicted the Christian situation in our time?

We are currently seeing an amazing expansion of the teaching and preaching of the Word of God across the world. We have moved into broad, sunlit uplands of opportunity which could not have been foreseen a generation ago. Conversation about Jesus Christ has changed from an embarrassed whisper to table talk among millions of people in America. The evidence grows on every hand that the message of the Bible has become an interesting topic to more people than anyone would have dared to imagine in our present world.

The ministry of evangelism has taken the form of millions gathering to hear the gospel of Jesus Christ in our generation. The message that "Christ died for our sins according to the Scriptures" has been presented to our society in numerous ways. Radio, television and the printed page carry the words of life in Christ to the ends of the earth. Reaching through formerly impenetrable walls of ignorance, prejudice and rejection, the message of Jesus Christ has touched more people in our time than in any similar period in the history of the church.

Time was, in the memory of many, when evangelistic preaching took the form of messages given to small but eager crowds, meeting in little auditoriums here and there. The ranks of believing Christians were made up of the common people. They gathered into gospel meetings from their pitiful economic and social circumstances to hear of Christ and His power to save. Believing, they were born again and became new creatures in Christ.

These new Christians went out with an eager testimony for the Savior, but the world took little note of these feeble beginnings of a new return to biblical truth on the part of the people who called themselves "fundamentalists."

All that has now changed. Orthodox, fundamental Christianity has come to the place of notice because of its numbers and enthusiasm. It has become a force to be reckoned with. The young people who heard the gospel from the consecrated, godly evangelists of yesterday have now moved into positions of leadership in business, the professions, the political world, and in the ever-growing avenues of opportunity now available in Christian service.

One of the reasons for the remarkable strength of Christianity in our present time has been the creative and effective youth work of the last generation. In many areas, the work of the Lord took the form of a high emphasis on the evangelism and training of young people. Leaders with a vision for tomorrow saw that the future was in youth, wearing tennis shoes and a T-shirt. It existed in young people who brushed back their unkempt hair and listened to the Bible. The future that those leaders dimly traced in that day is now the present. It is embodied in educated, talented, consecrated leadership in the world of the present that is so different from that of a generation ago. Few activities on the part of Christians in the last generation are now bearing greater dividends than that of reaching young people for Christ during those years.

There is no doubt that the present, thrilling expansion of Christian work has been greatly aided by the use of media, good organization, effective ideas, colorful promotion, and other modern methods. The communication developments of our time have certainly made it possible for the message of the gospel of Christ to be projected into areas that otherwise would be untouched. Methods and media, however, are not the real reason for the accomplishments of the gospel in our present world. The results which we see today are possible because of the foundations laid by the great leaders of the past. Our present harvest is being reaped because of the seed patiently sown by those who labored during an earlier, harder day. Yesterday's leaders did their work for Christ in the face of adversity, often in obscurity, and always with sacrifice. Many of them will not live to see the complete fulfillment of God's promise, "One sows and another reaps, but God gives the increase" (John 4:37; I Corinthians 3:7). This is harvest time, but there would be no harvest apart from those who led the way, who sowed in tears that we might reap in joy.

We are where we are today because of those noble soldiers who in the earlier battles took the high ground for our Great Commander. While every era of Christianity has produced spiritual noblemen who have accomplished great results for the Lord, the generation immediately past is surely exceptional in that regard. Christians of today work in the shadow of such men as Paul Rader, William P. Nicholson, William Pettingill, R. A. Torrey, William R. Newell, Louis Talbot, Harry Rimmer, Harry Ironside, Charles A. Fuller — the list could go on and on and reads like a Christian Hall of Fame. We stand for a moment of silence in memory of these great men of God and rejoice in the legacy of faith which they have produced as an inheritance for us.

There is one name that must be included on this list of

distinguished Christian leaders that has a very special and lasting meaning for many thousands of us. I refer to a man in whom God brought together in one remarkable personality the unusual combination of intellect, musical talent, personal charm, and indescribable discipline — all of which was capped by the crowning quality of life — faith in Jesus Christ as Savior and Lord.

This is a book about that man, about his message and his ministry. His name is Lance B. Latham.

Acknowledgments

To all who have made this book possible, my deepest thanks. The Awana secretarial staff played an important part in the preparation of this manuscript, typing and re-typing.

I am most grateful to Mrs. Marjorie Dold of Wilmette, Illinois who has applied the pencil and scissors and paste of her editing skills to the chapters of this volume.

We are grateful to the following people who responded to our requests for help and submitted resource material to be used in this biography:

Eleanor Antelo
Ruth Barker
Evangeline Lathem Buysse
Muriel Clifton
Jack Connor
Dr. Bob Cook
Linda Christensen
Merrill Dunlop
Peter Deyneka
Ed Dubisz
Ann Edgren
Dr. Ted Engstrom
Dr. Howard Ferrin
Ed Fiddler
Grace Frizane
Anna Gerali
Cal Hibbard
Anna Jones
Dr. Clarence Jones
Mrs. Charles Johnson

Dr. Torrey Johnson
Ken Johnston
Elizabeth Lathem
Dorothy Mackin
Dr. William McCarrell
Marshall Madsen
Dan Mielke
Art Rorheim
Mrs. Harry Saulnier
Howard Skinner
John Stahl
Phil Staalsen
Pastor Bob Swanson
Helen Lathem Taber
Elaine Townsend
Mrs. Donald VanderMolen
Charles Van Horn
Pastor Rich Wager
Walter Warfield

Introduction

The crowd was silent, tense, fascinated. Three thousand people leaned forward in their seats and listened, their attention gripped by a single person speaking into a microphone in the center of the gym floor. Looking at this improbable audience, one could notice smiles, nods of assent, occasional tears.

This captivated crowd was listening, but not to the plaintive notes of a blues singer. They were not watching the pulsating gyrations of a rock star. This was not a Hollywood production which commanded attention from the farthest reaches of the auditorium.

Before them was a young man who was bringing to them the simple story of his life. In his testimony, he told of past escapades in the streets of Chicago and his early brush with the police as he began to move toward a career of crime. He then testified that his life had been dramatically changed by discovering a wonderful message which he called "the gospel of the grace of God." He told the moving story of what Jesus Christ had done for him in sacrificing His life on Calvary's cross. He recounted that since that discovery and his faith in the Son of God, his life had never been the same again. His sins had been forgiven, the direction of his life changed. He was now a new creature because Christ had come to live within.

The occasion was the Awana Olympics, a program conducted under the growing ministry of the Awana Youth Association. Competition was keen as boys and girls had achieved in their handbooks to qualify for the athletic teams, and proud parents and friends cheered for the 300 team members and officials on the game floor. This crowd was watching just one of a hundred similar athletic and testimony programs which were being conducted that very month across the nation. The young man with the testimony had come to the same discovery that thousands of young people had made through the remarkable ministry of Awana. In becoming a Christian, he had joined the tens of thousands of youth who had already stepped out of the darkness of a hopeless past into the light of the gospel of Jesus Christ.

The crowd soon listened with the same intensity to an introduction being made by the evening's master of ceremonies, Mr. Art Rorheim. Rorheim, the director of the Awana Youth Association, made it clear that this was the most important introduction of the evening. He said, "Ladies and gentlemen, I know that we have all enjoyed this wonderful gathering. We have shared in the enthusiasm of this great crowd of teenagers as they participated in tonight's Olympic program. We have listened to the testimonies of boys and girls who have been saved as a result of hearing the gospel in their Awana Clubs, at Camp Awana, or another one of the many activities of the Awana program. We have been reminded that God has allowed us to see develop in our time a ministry that has reached out to several hundred thousand boys and girls who will be the leaders of tomorrow."

Rorheim continued, saying, "I am sure you know that this program did not happen by accident. Awana is the result of the labor and love of countless folks who have invested themselves, their time, their prayers, and their money to make this program go. Time does not allow us to say thank you to the great men and women who are a part of the miracle that is Awana.

"But tonight, "Art continued, "I want you to meet the man who above all others could be called the founding father of this ministry. In his heart many years ago was born a great concern for boys and girls and a consuming passion to see them won for Jesus Christ. Since the day of his own salvation he has given himself to no other purpose than to bring the gospel of the grace of God to as many people as possible. A ministry such as ours inevitably is built on a message and on a man. We know that message; it is the message of the finished work of Christ on the cross of Calvary. Tonight I want you to meet that man."

At this point, the words seemed to catch in Rorheim's throat. He grew pensive, saying, "I cannot introduce this gentleman without thanking God again for the day that he entered my life. My brother, in almost the last moments of his life, asked those who gathered about his hospital bed to pray for me because I was not a Christian. The man I want you to meet tonight was the human instrument who brought to pass the answer to my brother's prayer. Here is the one who led me to Christ, and whose enthusiasm for Christ became the early motivation of my life. Tonight, I want you to meet my pastor and friend, Lance B. Latham."

As the slight, agile gentleman, then in his eighty-fourth year of life, walked to the microphone, the crowd applauded with a quality that was more than appreciation. *It was love!* They were saying "thank you" not merely for his appearance that evening, but for his life, a life of selfless service for Christ and for them. Many in that auditorium had been saved when Lance preached the Word to them. Others knew that the threads of their spiritual heritage could be traced to this man who had

Lance Latham and Merrill Dunlop, a piano team ministering in the days of Paul Rader. They still play together as part of the annual four piano concerts at the North Side Gospel Center.

Doc with his White Shirt Brigade. The members of the group varied, but the musical message remained a blessing. Seeds planted by Doc in the hearts of the boys years ago are still bearing fruit.

interrupted their downward path with an unforgettable message of the gospel of the grace of God. This message had come in the form of a sermon, a Bible lesson, a radio broadcast, or even a faithful hand laid on their shoulder with a loving reminder of their spiritual need. They were applauding the man who had become the spiritual father to many of them.

Lance Latham began his message that evening with a self-effacing remark and a note of appreciation for the evening's program and for those who had made it possible. Despising "snappy sermon starters," he immediately called their attention to a verse from his favorite passage in the Bible, Romans, chapter three.

The message that evening spoke of many things; of sin, of righteousness, of judgment to come. It referred to the "old Tab days," an experience at Camp Awana, and to the White Shirt Brigade. It used an occasional homely illustration to clarify a spiritual point. Those who heard Lance Latham for the first time wondered if indeed this was the man of whom they had been told so much. They experienced that evening the oft-repeated fact that no one message could fulfill those images which had been built about his ministry over a lifetime, images of a man who had become a legend in his own time. Nevertheless, they knew that they were listening to one who knew them and who *cared*. Fascinated, they were attracted to the remarkable spirit of this man. They asked themselves again the question, "What kind of a man is Lance Latham, and what is the road of life which he has followed that has brought him to this hour? What has been built into the fiber of this man that has made it possible for him to so move the lives of many? Who is Lance Latham?"

1

I Always Knew
He was a Genius

The man sat straight as a ramrod in his cushionless, straight-backed chair. His patrician head was held high above a starched Oxford collar as he listened carefully to the recitations of the boy standing before him. The house was beginning to stir with the sounds and aromas of breakfast. But no matter, the business of the moment was to hear with exactitude the lessons of the day from this boy. Nothing must interrupt his responsibility to preside over the training, education, and discipline of his son.

The stern figure who presided over this early morning lesson review was Pastor Abraham Lathem. This white-haired gentleman was, by the testimony of all who knew him, no ordinary man. The Presbyterian manse over which he presided sheltered his wife and four children, a family whose remarkable qualities were being honed by the stern, Puritan discipline that today would be called "the old school." Abraham Lathem was the most powerful early directional force in the life of his son, and Lance was later to remember with gratefulness the influence of godly parents in his life.

The life of Lance Brenton Lathem began on the

1

twenty-first day of March in the year 1894 in the little city of Dentonville, Pennsylvania. His father, Rev. Abraham Lathem, was pastor of the Third Presbyterian Church of Chester, Pennsylvania. Lance Lathem (the spelling was later changed to Latham), born into the home of a pastor, was to learn the qualities that would be developed in him as an instrument—a lance—for the Lord.

Standing before his father to recite his daily lessons in an early morning hour, Lance Latham could hardly foresee the good that this was doing him. He remembers, "Every morning during my entire school life I was called at four fifty-five to be downstairs at five o'clock sharp. The lesson which had been personally and thoroughly heard the night before by Father until just-about perfection was attained, was heard again until time to go to school. Time was allowed for breakfast and the memorizing of two Bible verses each day, along with review! The work of the week was reviewed on the Saturday morning following, from six o'clock until noon. Being second in my class was not my achievement, but that of an indomitable, persevering father."

"Indomitable and persevering," these were Lance's words for it. For Abraham Lathem, the training of his son was a responsibility which was placed upon him by God. He believed with a perfect faith that children were "an heritage of the Lord" and that settled it. We are not in this world to play and drift, we are here to accomplish a purpose that has been placed upon us by the will of God. Like it or not, awakening his son at four fifty-five in the morning was a part of that responsibility. Through the eyes of faith, he could perhaps foresee the wide and eternal dividends that would be produced in the life of the child who stood before him reciting his verses. Abraham Lathem was later to find that not only through his own ministry but through the life of his son, his faith would be spoken of through the whole world. The disciplines of those days were to be translated through the person of this willowy boy to a whole generation of young people.

The remembrance of his father will never leave the mind of Lance Latham. Recalling those formative years, Lance writes, "When I think of beginnings, there comes immediately to mind a faithful and devoted father and mother. Father had no other desire than to live for God and to train his son in that direction."

Abraham Lathem had reasons for this attitude which grew out of his early life. In his youth, Abraham knew only the stern, disciplined life that came from scratching out a living on a small farm in western Pennsylvania. Before Abraham was five years of age he lost both his father and mother. We can be sure that his young, inquiring mind faced many questions about God, eternity, the purpose of life, and the reason why these events had befallen him. Deep and sometimes unanswerable as these questions were, they could not keep him from coming by faith to Jesus Christ and receiving Him as personal Savior. This he did at the age of twelve. From that moment on, his life, as described by his son, was "utterly uncompromising, never two-faced." Abraham Lathem learned from his experiences in nineteenth century America and from the Word of God the simple certainties of life and death. He therefore had no other ambition for his son than that the same life and attitudes should be built into the fiber of this young man's being.

Throughout his ministry as a pastor, Abraham Lathem saw these deep spiritual convictions take root in the lives of his people. He was pastor of Chester, Pennsylvania's Third Presbyterian Church for more than thirty-five years. His forceful preaching of the faith "once delivered to the saints" gathered seeking hearts to hear the Word from every direction. Remembering

3

those days, one of his parishioners reports, "It grew to be a great church of over 1,600 members under a pastor who had a firm belief in the old faith, implicit trust in the infallability of the Word of God, and belief in scriptural separation from worldly practices and habits."

What Abraham Lathem believed about the sober responsibility of raising a family in the nurture and admonition of the Lord, he also believed about a church. He was never content therefore to merely conduct a service on Sunday morning. This, in his mind, was only the beginning of a church's responsibility. His church instituted a full program of activities for his people that would make their involvement in the Third Presbyterian Church a total experience. He was sure that it was the responsibility of the church to cause every individual member to be thoroughly grounded in the Word of God.

Besides the three regular services of the week, one of the methods which he used to accomplish this scriptural grounding was the summer Bible school. The summer Bible classes at the church hardly resembled what we normally understand as the vacation Bible school of our time. It was virtually a Bible institute program in which a curriculum was set up that would be a credit to any Bible college today. The five-week-long schedule for the students included studies in Christian living, Bible history, Bible geography, and the inevitable review of the Shorter Catechism, then taught to all Presbyterian youth. The program included a major emphasis on Bible memorization, and the closing exercises featured recitations of whole Bible chapters. One of them, for the tenth graders, called for the recitation of the entire passages of John 14:1-21 and Romans 8:1-10. This demanding schedule attracted as many as seven hundred young people and adults from the Chester area every summer.

One of Pastor Lathem's parishioners recalls, "As he

4

observed the falling away of members from the denomination, he felt the need of rooting and grounding the people in the Word of God, which resulted in the formation of the summer Bible school. The school originated about 1912 and was held Monday through Friday from nine o'clock to noon for five weeks each summer. Each year, Abraham Lathem began preparing for the school in February by getting teachers. In March he contacted the pupils who had attended the preceding year, and community canvasses were made for new pupils. The Lord privileged him to conduct forty-three of the schools. He was eighty-eight years of age when conducting the forty-third school. (The sixty-sixth school was held in the summer of 1978.)" The summer Bible school programs of our time could be compared with interest to those which were organized by Abraham Lathem.

It was this discipline and godly concern for a spiritual foundation in the lives of young people which became the environment of the youth of Lance Latham. Lance remembers all of this with gratefulness, saying about his father, "His disciplined regularity was shown in our never missing morning worship, the reciting of one-half of the Presbyterian Shorter Catechism every morning, and our learning of two verses of Scripture every morning. No wonder I had learned three books of the Bible by the time I was seven years old — Romans, the Gospel of John, and the Epistle of James, reciting each in its entirety at one sitting."

Four children were born into the home of Abraham and Elizabeth Lathem; Elizabeth, Helen, Lance and Evangeline. In remembering the dominant influence of Abraham Lathem, we must also not forget the glow that was added to the fireside of the Lathem home by Lance's godly mother.

Elizabeth McKeag Lathem also came from staunch,

5

Abraham and Elizabeth Lathem, parents of Lance and staunch believers in the scriptural promise, "Train up a child in the way he should go: and when he is old, he will not depart from it" [Proverbs 22:6].

Abraham Lance Lathem, PH.D., D.D., staunch defender of the faith, invested himself in the lives of his children and the children of his parishioners.

Third Presbyterian Church and manse in Chester, Pennsylvania, Lance's childhood home where he began memorizing Scripture under the strict tutelage of his father.

Lance at the age of eight

Lance and his sisters, Elizabeth, Helen and Evangeline

Oct. 27, 1901.

Lance Brenton Lathem,—
    This book is presented
to you for having memo-
ized and recited correctly
The Gospel by st. John,
The Epistle to the Romans,
The Epistle of James, each
entire on one occasion,
        Abraham L. Lathem

Presbyterian stock. Her early interest in music and her sensitive spirit made her a great source of attraction to the purposeful, practical Abraham Lathem. Already sensing his calling into the ministry, he chose for himself a wife who would stand by his side as a great spiritual credential. Elizabeth Lathem's winsome, feminine spirit was a happy counterpart to that of her rock-ribbed Presbyterian husband. Together they became a mutual inspiration and example to their children, bringing them up in the nurture and admonition of the Lord.

While there are many influences that fashion our personalities and our destinies, that of our parents is usually the greatest. In the life of Lance Latham, this was certainly the case. His sisters also remember him with boundless affection and have many moving recollections of Lance as a boy at home. One of them told us, "When Lance was about three years old, Mother began teaching him the piano. Very shortly she used the hymnbook as the basis for Lance's piano lessons. She would call out page numbers of hymns for Lance to play and she soon noticed that he did not turn to the numbers, for he knew the hymn relating to the number and could play it by heart. He also had learned how to read, spell, and do first-grade arithmetic by the age of three. When he was four years of age, he recited the 107 answers to The Shorter Catechism, asking the questions as well."

Evangeline mentions, "As a tiny child, words from the Bible or from Father's sermons were already deeply embedded in Lance's mind. When Mother asked Lance, when he was about the age of five, to entertain a wrinkled and aged member of the congregation while she made tea, she returned to hear Lance asking politely, 'Miss Binksen, were you present when Noah was building the ark?' "

As in the life of any child, there were amusing incidents that come from a child's point of view. The ready young mind of Lance Latham as a child would inevitably make the connection that was expressed by one of these incidents. Evangeline recalls, "In walking along the streets of Philadelphia, Quakers were seen in some numbers with their special dress. Whenever these people came nearby, dressed in black and looking very sober, Lance would hold Mother's hand tightly and act afraid. Once his mother questioned his response and he said, 'These are the people who bring the earthquakes!'"

Elizabeth also adds her recollections of Lance as a small child. She recalls, "His education began at age three with his father as his instructor. He soon was studying language in detail. When he reached the place where he could write declensions and conjugations, one mistake meant rewriting the whole paragraph." She also recalls that "his mother was his first piano teacher. By the age of five, he could play any hymn in the hymnal and he was the pianist for the primary department in our church." A Sunday School that has as its regular pianist a boy who is five years old is a unique one indeed. The leader could ask for almost any hymn in the hymnbook and his five-year-old prodigy pianist could play it from memory without even looking for it in the book.

Lance's remarkable ability to memorize Scripture was also noted by his Sunday School teachers. He always could be counted upon not only to memorize the regular verses but to move into the extra lists entitled "Additional Bible Study." It is interesting that most who remember him in those days often mention repeatedly that "he could recite the 107 questions and answers of The Shorter Catechism by the age of five."

We may be sure that his parents took due notice of the unusual child whom God had given them. They would never use the word "prodigy" in his presence, but in their private discussions, they voiced their concern about his education. They were sure that his ability placed upon them a great responsibility to see this unusual mind have an opportunity for education equal to its capacity. Here Evangeline recalls, "Taking these things into consideration, Father presented him to the headmaster of the William Penn Charter School in Philadelphia. This man asked the young child many questions and was astonished at his knowledge. He was then delighted to have Lance enter the school as the very youngest student. So impressed was this man that he said he would like to also meet the mother of this remarkable child."

Helen Lathem Taber, Lance's sister, adds a most interesting note in her recollection of her brother. "Everyone noticed his remarkable learning ability. He took the twelve years of schooling in six years at Penn Charter where he had a scholarship." By the age of nine, Lance was studying the Greek New Testament, and Helen recalls that at age ten, he was able to read from the Greek for evening devotions.

The six years spent at Penn Charter School were years of development of the mind for Lance Latham. Here this special student developed his remarkable learning ability in the study of English, German, Greek, and in it all, logical thinking. His musical ability was developing through his studies at the Philadelphia Conservatory. Members of his family recall the music he mastered by the twelfth year of his life, saying, "Listening to Lance play Bach, Beethoven, and Liszt's Hungarian Rhapsodies was something like heaven!" By the time Lance Latham moved into his teenage years, he carried with him an educational background that would be difficult to duplicate in these modern times.

One wonders how many young people are trapped in today's educational system, so influenced by liberal thinking, who will not recover from an early inattention to the basics. We may rejoice that in the providence of

God, Lance Latham was shackled with no such educational limitation. By age 13, he graduated summa cum laude from Penn Charter. The same year, he took the entrance exams given by the University of Pennsylvania and his marks were the highest on record at that time. Because of Lance's youth, his father and mother thought it best that he should stay for another year at Penn Charter. Here he made another scholastic record, and at the end of the year, was offered a full scholarship to Haverford College.

Lance Latham was now entering into the teenage era of his life. His background in both secular and religious education was impeccable. He knew the Bible, the classics, languages, and also the world of music. He had considered the basic questions of life a thousand times over and knew the answers that were given by the men of history. Despite all of this, he was still pressed with the basic questions having to do with the purpose of life, the meaning of existence, the personal reality of God — the questions that every young and emergent mind faces and to which it must find the answers.

Nevertheless, the foundation had been well set in the life of Lance Latham by the influence, teaching, and example of his godly parents and also by his educational background. For the rest of his life, Lance would be known as the earliest riser, the hardest worker, and the most disciplined student of any group which knew him. He was instantly ready to perform any task, and brought to it his well-developed habits of thinking and action which never failed through all of his life. He has always been known by this writer and others as one who could do the thinking of two men and the work of three. He has had little patience with those who slept too long or neglected to attack a problem forthrightly. By the time he was five years old, these capacities were well set in his life and personality.

No one who knew him ever doubted that he was a perfect illustration of the promise of Scripture, "Train up a child in the way he should go: and when he is old, he will not depart from it" (Proverbs 22:6). For all of his life, Lance never failed to remind parents and congregations to whom he preached of their opportunity and great responsibility toward their own children. He never considered his own personal background as anything unusual, but the normal, predictable result of the concern, the love, and the discipline which was placed upon him in his formative years.

During the years of his later ministry, Lance Latham would remind a generation of adults and young people of the value of discipline, Scripture memorizing, and faithful practice at the thing in which they wished to excel. His advice could never be discounted, for everyone knew that he was speaking out of his own experience and was himself an illustration of the personal discipline that he called for in the lives of others. For the rest of his life, Lance Latham was to be the illustration used by parents when they spoke to their own children about what study, duty, and diligence could accomplish in a life. More than many other things, these early experiences were to enable Lance Latham to "endure hardness, as a good soldier of Jesus Christ" (II Timothy 2:3).

During those early years, that discipline enabled him to become the outstanding student at Penn Charter School where he graduated with honors at the age of thirteen. So it was that in his fourteenth year, he stood at the gates of Haverford College, the youngest member of its freshman class.

When asked about all these things, his mother said, "I always knew that he was a genius."

2

A College Education

"Welcome to Haverford College!

"I know that you young men have come from many places, and you are now here to expand your minds and face all the brilliant possibilities that are before you in these exciting days. We're happy to have you with us, and I know that together we will discover the realities of life from the teachings of the Bible and other equally marvelous sources of knowledge that are available to us today."

Young Lance Latham, fourteen years of age and the youngest student of the freshman class, listened with interest to these words of welcome from Dr. Rufus Jones, distinguished professor of Bible and history at one of America's finest Presbyterian schools. Coming to Haverford brought a great sense of fulfillment for him, for here he believed he would discover the answers to the questions of life, and here would be revealed to him the purpose for which he was made. Lance Latham looked forward to his college experience with understandable anticipation. His mind, which was more perceptive than that of normal fourteen-year-olds, would soon be reaching out to grasp the further knowledge that Haverford would have available to him.

Moving into his college experience, young Lance soon suspected that there was a troubling difference in the religious faith believed in this institution from that which he had learned under the regular expository preaching of his orthodox Presbyterian father. There was something about the way the Bible was taught, and the degree of respect given to modern thought, which suggested that traditional orthodox Christianity was not in fact the faith believed in this school.

Jones and others delivered lectures that repeatedly contained this unorthodox slant.

"I know that many of you have come from churches which told you those pleasant stories about Adam and Eve being created out of the dust of the ground in the image of God. Up until now, you have looked at the Bible as the inspired Word of God. According to your best understanding, you believe that Jesus Christ is 'the Son of God' and that He proved this by real miracles which He accomplished in the sight of many. Now, believe me, it's not my purpose to shake the faith of any of you, but I would like to remind you that if you want to be an intelligent Christian, you will think again about these archaic views and consider some of the more modern conclusions which our present level of scholarship has led us to believe today."

With these and other words, the professor introduced to his class a whole new view of Christianity. This set of ideas called "religious liberalism" had begun to make its way into the teaching of this Presbyterian school. Lance Latham listened with astonishment as he heard for the first time that the Bible probably contained many myths and was not necessarily factually true. Jesus Christ was the Son of God, they acknowledged, but in much the same sense that all of us are sons of God when we see Jehovah as our Universal Heavenly Father. According to these professors, Jesus Christ certainly spoke wisely as one of the world's greatest teachers, but His words have been explained and corrected by other

16

wise men. In the minds and the mouths of these professors, the Bible became a human book, and Christianity was thought of as being one of the great religions of the world. The new liberalism was underway in America.

For many of the students in those days, the shock was very great since after all, Haverford was one of America's finest colleges. Its solemn, ivy-covered buildings sheltered 160 students and 25 full-time professors who lived on the grounds. The respected faculty included such notables as Francis B. Gummere, the greatest authority on Shakespeare who lived in the world at that time. The professors at Haverford presented views which were difficult for the students to withstand. These were men of academic credentials, but they now represented the new religious liberalism. In the minds of their students, the result was a variety of responses from resentment to acceptance.

Lance Latham, always thoughtful about these things, began to compare the new religion preached in the name of Christianity to the old faith which he had learned in his father's church. The difference was clear to this young man of fourteen, even though the difference between Christianity and liberalism has been less clear to many who have heard the liberal view in our time. Lance, for instance, wrote an interesting conclusion to an exam which he took in a Bible literature course. "I have written all this because I have to, but I don't believe a word of it." Because of his early Bible teaching in the home of his parents, Lance had no difficulty passing the exam with a perfect grade. His contempt for the liberal theology involved, however, was expressed by the closing statement of his exam paper.

The response from the teacher was most interesting. Lance recalls that he said, "I read your note at the end of your exam. You'll soon discover that modern theology is

17

finding that the new view of the Bible is enabling modern man to find it more acceptable to logical thinking. When you get a little older and a little wiser, you'll be looking at all of this very differently." So the distinguished professor spoke to his brilliant but resentful student in his office after the exam. He saw in young Lance Latham a mind worth capturing with this whole new view of biblical inspiration, human nature, and the Word of God. He dared to hope that this young mind could be enrolled in the cause of the new liberalism which he himself represented.

Young Lance's answer settled the argument. The lad, looking up at the professor, said, "Well, my dad is about as old and as wise as you are, and he still believes that the Bible is the Word of God and that Jesus Christ is God's only begotten Son. So, I am going to stick with the old faith." Following this retort, the professor had nothing to say. Lance said, "In my years at this lovely college I met no more than six men who claimed to be saved." Many young men in those days were subverted by the new views of the Christian religion. They went on to serve in the religious world, laboring through a life-long and impotent ministry because their faith had been lost in their college years, a situation that is doubtless being repeated in many denominational and secular schools today. Lance Latham frequently rejoiced that his experience was different from these many, for the training of the past enabled him to retain a correct doctrinal view. Although Lance was not to come to Christ until seven years later, the early training and acceptance of Scripture as the infallible Word of God enabled him to weather the storm of what he remembers as "deadly, soul-destroying teaching."

Lance's college experience was to leave a noticeable mark on him. For the rest of his life, he was always reluctant to recommend schools of higher learning to eager students who wished to pursue more education in order to serve their Savior. He mistrusted education, reminding us always that God has promised to destroy the wisdom of the wise, and to bring to nothing the understanding of the prudent.

For the balance of his life as well, Lance Latham was to retain a particular sensitivity to the truth of the gospel and an instant recognition of any tendency toward a liberal alternative. "Liberalism has become the great curse of Christianity," Lance Latham said, "for it makes people believe that they are truly Christians, but it leaves out the heart of the gospel, the deity of Christ, and the finished work of Calvary's cross. This is *the fatal omission* which makes liberalism merely a sweet religion which sounds good on the surface but ends up destroying the soul." For Lance, religious liberalism was another religion entirely from the faith of historic Christianity. He later became an admirer of the distinguished scholar Gresham Machen, who wrote the best book in print to point up this precise problem, *Christianity and Liberalism.*

In the midst of it all, however, Lance remembers some humorous aspects of his studies at Haverford. "The hurried, last-minute preparation was evidence that not only in this course, but in other courses, exams of previous years were saved and passed on to the next class so that none would be wearied or suffer a nervous breakdown through overwork. Many of the questions were repeated in the Bible exam. One of two difficult questions seemed sure to be asked; never both, however, in one Bible exam. They were, 'Distinguish between the major and minor prophets,' and 'Give the names of the kings of Israel.' The boys would select one from these two subjects, the one more likely to be asked. On one particular occasion of the final exam, a group of overworked students selected the second as the one to study, 'The kings of Israel.' To their horror, the question asked was 'Distinguish between the major and the minor prophets.' One brilliant freshman, not to be embarrassed, answered, 'God forbid that I should draw invidious distinctions between these holy men. But here are the names of the kings of Israel.' His convictions were respected." One wonders if the brilliant freshman was not Lance Latham himself.

College life, however, includes a whole set of experiences by which we are often enabled to discover who we are. So it was that Lance Latham also recalls, "Rooming in Haverford with two wonderful young men, one the captain of the track and soccer teams and the other the captain of the gym team, I had a part in many Saturday nights of entertaining the members of the college teams. One night I especially remember, ten members of the University of Pennsylvania football team were the guests."

Lance continues describing this occasion, "In those days, they enjoyed classical music. I played piano for them for a half hour or so. At my right sat the captain of the University of Pennsylvania team, a fine-looking 220-pound fullback. He listened intently and said to me, 'I would give up my football if I could only do what you are doing.' I said, 'No, you wouldn't ... I would give up this to be like you.' He answered, 'No! I mean what I say. What you have is far better than anything I have.'"

That brief conversation had a far-reaching effect on the life of Lance Latham. He was himself a competitor in track and field events and would certainly be called an expert at the horizontal bar. He was a fine player on the tennis court and exercised daily all of his life to keep in athletic trim. So Lance Latham, the scholar-musician, had a great respect for athletic prowess. Since he was slight of build, we can even suspect that there was a touch of hero-worship in his mind as he caught the roar of the crowd and watched the competitors in an athletic event carry the baton to the finish line for first place. Until this time, however, the words of encouragement and motivation had come chiefly from his father and his family.

He had now come to the time when he must decide if his talents had relative, comparative worth in a world apart from the Presbyterian manse.

He writes, "That encouraging word from the star football player inspired me. Maybe I had something worthwhile. *In one moment, he did for me what ten years of teachers had failed to do. He gave me ambition.*"

So came the golden moment in the life of Lance Latham, the birth of ambition.

Many a college educational program in these days could valuably hear one of Lance's recollections of that experience in those days at Haverford. He said, "We fear this is true too often in our colleges and seminaries, even where the Lord is magnified. There is *exhortation, perfection, desire to excel, but no thrill!* There is correct definition, grasp of theology, orderly presentation, but that which encourages and convicts is sadly lacking. 'Though I speak ... and have not love, I am nothing.'"

The results have been far-reaching. Along with thousands of others, I can say that I have never heard Lance Latham speak without there being *something of the thrill* in his remarks. He has never preached merely static doctrine, cold theology. He has swayed many an audience with that secret emotion of the spirit, moving them beyond what they ever expected to be at the beginning of a meeting. Many have experienced in their own hearts something of what must have been the sentiment of the disciples when they said, "Did not our heart burn within, us while he talked with us by the way, and while he opened to us the Scriptures?" (Luke 24:32). The disciples, of course, were speaking about Jesus Christ on

21

the road to Emmaus. Many of us are very sure that this same Lord Jesus has used some of His followers to produce much that same result in the minds and hearts of those who hear.

There came at this point into Lance Latham's life a determination to give himself to the development of his already remarkable talent which was to come to magnificent flower in the following years of life. A major portion of the life of Lance Latham came into beautiful focus when this young man with a determined spirit said, "I will devote myself to music."

For Lance, decision was always followed by action. No one ever knew him to give himself to dreaming, drifting, or groping for a result. He set himself on an immediate course of action because of his decision, "I will devote myself to music."

He described his course of action, "I went to Mauritz Leefson, the director of the Philadelphia Conservatory of Music, and told him that I wanted him to teach me. He had many pupils and did not desire to add another, and so he tried to induce me to go to his brother. But his brother was not the director of the conservatory, he did not have a goatee, he did not have grand pianos in his studio ... no, he would not do!

"So Mauritz Leefson accepted me. My fifth lesson was one I will not forget. Each week I was supposed to work on the usual Bach, an exercise book, and a selection of new music. I was playing from the exercise book when suddenly my teacher removed the music. I was unable to proceed. He said, 'You have not practiced.' I had practiced and as decently as I was able. I told him so. He said sternly, the goatee vibrating feverishly from side to side ... 'Don't you contradict me! If you had really practiced, you would know this by heart. Don't come back unless you have everything memorized! I realized I could memorize every note. I wanted that teacher!"

In these, his own words, Lance gives us a marvelous index into his own personality. Having decided that he would give himself to music, Lance would settle for nothing less than the very best instruction. How fearful must have been the moment when Leefson told him never to come back. Here, Lance discovered that it is possible to make nearly infinite demands upon ourselves and produce a result. Again the lessons of discipline that began at the age of three at his father's knee were beginning to pay dividends in this growing life.

Lance Latham was later to organize training programs for thousands of young people. His father and his demanding music teacher invested within him some of the convictions which were later to be wrought in the lives of so many others. Lance's lifelong conviction was that the Christian life was a thing to be disciplined and tailored under the matchless training of God Himself. Without training, all enthusiasm and mere inspiration go for nothing.

So it was that at Haverford a vital new element was injected into the life of Lance Latham — ambition. Ambition — later to become godly ambition — must be added to knowledge and talent for results to be produced. He brought to his college studies a wealth of knowledge and also the same discipline that had mainly characterized his early years. Few teachers have the opportunity in a lifetime of teaching to have a student who comes to college already accomplished in Greek, German, English, and music. Education for Lance Latham had not been basket weaving ... it was the development of the most precious entity in the life of any human being, his mind.

When speaking with Lance, one receives the impression that he could, if he so desired, finish a sentence before it was completed by the speaker. For all of life, he was to be impatient with ambiguity. He had little sympathy with those even in pulpits who would preach lengthy sermons of circuitous logic and false conclusions. For him, there would always be the objective, unchangeable value of final knowledge based on the Word of God with which all our reasoning must begin.

Liberalism, modern ideas and avant-garde thinking never had the slightest appeal for Lance. He could instantly see through the shallow thinking, the porous logic of the new views that had started to come upon the religious scene. For him, liberalism was naive and irresponsible, believed by shallow preachers and preached to shallow parishioners.

So, during his college years, music moved near to the center of the life of Lance Latham. Preserved news clippings from that time mention that "Lance B. Latham, noted concert pianist, will play..." Fliers for the best of concerts announced, "Lance Latham at the Organ." This eager young musician was becoming the toast of the Philadelphia area. His life was moving in the direction of the concert stage.

Through the years, he was invited to conduct concerts in churches and public halls across the Philadelphia area, and he was widely acclaimed as the young man who could do anything on the organ and piano. A growing circle of admirers agreed that the world of music would open before him and he would be its master. Indeed, he paid his way through college not only by scholarships and tutoring, but especially with his memorable recitals at the organ and piano.

Inevitably he was, during those days, offered many attractive opportunities to continue in the musical world both in the United States and abroad. Lance Latham, the amazing young musician from Haverford, would surely be known to his generation.

Indeed he was, but in a way different from what anyone could have predicted.

3

The Divine Captive

Once again came that magic moment.

The crowd listened to the opening numbers of the concert with an increasing sense of incredulity. They could hardly believe their ears! They gradually leaned forward and pressed their attention upon a single scene. The young pianist seemed to breathe a part of his life through his fingers onto the keyboard. Those supple hands and flying fingers issued in music which seemed to be not of this world. The attitude of the crowd changed from incredulity to amazed acceptance. Then came that moment without which a concert is not a concert — total immersion. The people forgot themselves and became lost in the classic piano artistry of the faultless player who translated the printed notes of Beethoven, Bach and Liszt into a form of music which each person in the crowd was sure he had never heard before.

Many were sure that the name of Lance B. Latham would make its way to the top of the concert world. They knew that they were privileged to listen to the early piano presentations of an artist whose career was assured. They were sure that the music and the man had found each other in the person of this keyboard prodigy.

Lance had also made this decision. He would give himself to music and that would be his life. His decision was strengthened by the assurances of the capacity

Lance, even as a young man, exhibited the poise and quiet determination which have characterized his entire life.

The piano has always played an important part in Lance's life and his talent has been dedicated to the glory of God.

crowds who attended his concerts. Philadelphians were not that easy to impress. Their response seemed to confirm the decision that Lance had made the wisest choice in pursuing the music that had been his obvious talent since the age of five.

With this confidence, Lance entered the twenty-first year of his life. He had graduated from Haverford, and in a year of post-graduate studies, received his MA degree in biology at the age of 17. The "summa cum laude" on his graduation certificate was simply the predictable result of the intensity with which he had invested himself in his education, just as he did in all other things. His years of service as a teaching fellow had strengthened his personality. He began accepting invitations for concerts and piano recitals with increasing frequency. The world of music was to be his life!

And a most interesting world it was! The year of 1915 was a most provocative one in many ways. The clouds of World War I were beginning to gather and would soon break in fury on the continent of Europe. Across America young men would soon be singing "Over There" and donning uniforms of khaki and helmets of steel to go to the front and save the world for democracy.

Along with political unrest came new ideas about other things. Marxism was gathering its forces for the conquest and capture of Czarist Russia. The pressures were mounting that would result in the Communist revolution, the Eight Days that would shake the world.

The world of religion had also lost its traditional simplicity. Even the dependable, historic Presbyterianism of Havorford College had given way to the new, liberal theology of the German rationalists. The old orthodoxy had been assaulted by the modernism of that day and religious institutions were one by one crumbling before the new tide. The battle for Christian truth was being lost in the established educational institutions as well as the great denominations of that day. Protestant Christianity, from this point on, would divide into liberal and conservative theologies. It would become a humanistic religion on one hand and bring a new emphasis on divine truth on the other. The alternatives of divine revelation and human reason were being cast as the great division of our century. From this point on, every religious institution and every person would be called upon to choose between human reason and divine revelation. They would choose between the new liberalism and the old faith.

Those battle lines were being formed in the neart of Lance Latham. Despite his external appearance of confidence in his convictions and in his choice that music was to be the purpose of his life, the mind of Lance Latham knew no such finality. There, two major religious influences contended for supremacy.

One was the teaching that he had learned under the stern orthodoxy of Abraham Lathem. On this side of his mind and heart, the authority of Scripture, the deity of Christ, the sinfulness of man, and the salvation of God stood firm. The Scriptures which he had memorized in his father's early morning sessions continued to recite themselves in his inquiring mind. The truth of historic Christianity as learned in his orthodox Presbyterian background was the foundation on which his boyhood thinking had been built.

On the other side of his mind he reviewed the liberalism of Haverford College. These modern views had now begun to take hold in schools and churches and were not to be ignored. At this critical point in life, these ideas could not be ignored in the mind of Lance Latham. The liberalism of Rufus Jones and the casual attitude toward truth held by the other professors had not been without their effect on him. Lance confesses that in his college years he hardly opened his Bible to review the

29

precepts of his parents. The years were spent in the academic world, and little attention was paid to his spirit.

The consequence of all of this was that the questions of life still remained, and above all there was yet unsettled the question of personal salvation. No one could have memorized the Bible as Lance Latham did, and listened to the preaching to which he was exposed, and then find it easy to forget. Consequently, in the twenty-first year of his life, Lance Latham was a bright, externally satisfied young man who still carried within him a needy heart. Lance was facing the fact that no man can spend his life reviewing alternatives; he must make a choice. Until this time, no one had pressed upon him the absolute imperative of a decision for Christ. He knew that the Scripture said, "Ye must be born again," but this young, preoccupied mind had not yet been pressed with the issue of being saved or lost for all of eternity.

Then came William P. Nicholson!

Nicholson was an evangelist. His ministry was part of a new tide that was rising in America which seemed to be a divine response to the liberalism and deadness of the established churches. Scholarly and articulate preachers of the gospel were beginning to lift a forceful voice in the United States and across the world. Many chose the daring step of areawide evangelistic campaigns. They would gather the finest musical talent, rent the largest halls in American cities and towns, and fill them with eager listeners. Leaflets were distributed by the thousands. People were invited to come and hear the preaching of the Word of God. Cooperating in these great crusades were denominational churches which remained true to the faith and newer, smaller churches which had been formed in many places. Composed of people who wanted to return to the fundamentals of the faith, these new, fundamental churches cooperated enthusiastically with evangelistic crusades in the hope of spiritual revival. Thousands of Christians who believed in the changeless Word of God prayed that God would not leave Himself without a witness. They prayed for revival. They reached up holy hands to the Lord, praying in brokenness before God for a new, gracious working of the Holy Spirit. They knew that only showers of blessing from on high could turn the tide of liberalism, worldliness, immorality in society, and all the other ills that beset mankind. They had no confidence in an impotent social gospel that promised to alter society by other means than salvation from sin and regeneration by the Holy Spirit. The Christians of that day, true to the Word of God, placed their confidence in the Lord alone. They prayed that God would raise up men who would preach the Word with power from on high. In answer to these prayers, William P. Nicholson came to Chester, Pennsylvania for an evangelistic crusade.

The Third Presbyterian Church and Abraham Lathem, along with other churches in the community, cooperated fully with the crusade. Believers from every background came to sing the old hymns of the faith and say "amen" to the preaching of the Word of God. So great was the enthusiasm for the Chester crusade that it couldn't be stopped. It was originally planned to last for six weeks and then was extended to ten. William P. Nicholson, anointed of the Lord, tirelessly preached the gospel for two and a half months, every night of the week except Saturday. The auditorium was filled night after night in that glorious revival. Nicholson preached for a solid hour his great expository messages from the Scriptures. In those meetings, he took an entire chapter of the Bible and preached on it in great detail. He examined the moral nature of man and his sinful offense to the holiness of God. Conviction came upon the hearts and minds of people and great numbers came, confessing

31

Jesus Christ as their personal Savior. He delivered expositions of Scripture on every major theme in the New Testament. He analyzed the need of the sinful heart from every possible point of view. He preached for two weeks before giving an evangelistic invitation, carefully laying the groundwork so that no one could misunderstand the great doctrines of sin, the atonement of Christ, justification by faith, and the responsibility of every man to receive the gospel as the only basis for eternal life. No wonder so many came to the Savior, for such preaching is the kind God uses to bring devastating conviction to the sinful heart.

One such heart was that of Lance Latham, the Presbyterian preacher's son. He attended nearly every one of those meetings, listening night after night to this remarkable evangelist and his expositions of Holy Scripture. There arose in his mind the acute consciousness that every man is a sinner in need of the righteousness of God. He knew that the Bible taught the undeniable doctrine of original sin, but of course that is a far cry from personal conviction of sin.

"Who is that amazing pianist? In all my travels I have never heard such music."

So said Nicholson after hearing young Lance play a special piano number. He inquired as to the identity of this remarkable pianist. He came to the son of Abraham Lathem, one of the sponsors of the crusade, and said, "You must join our team as our pianist." So an invitation was extended to Lance Latham that was to establish the course of his life. Lance felt surprised and complimented and his heart was drawn to this remarkable preacher of the gospel and the message he had heard him present so many times. Lance Latham said, "Yes." He would be happy to travel in the evangelistic party of William P. Nicholson, playing the piano for those great crusades.

Lance writes of that day, saying, "In God's mercy,

Saved for Aye

Howard Jones

Lance B. Latham

The night of sin and death is end - ed, The light from Cal-va-ry I
Night of sin is end-ed, Light from

see; And all the shad-ows have de-part - ed,
Cal - va - ry; Shad - ows have de-part - ed,
Shad - ows part - ed,

Glo - - rious day! For - ev - er-more in end-less
Glo-rious day of joy and glad-ness! Ev - - - er

Now
glo - ry, For - ev - er-more in fade-less day;
end - less glo - ry, Ev - - - er fade - less day;
day;

My song of songs will be the sto - - ry, Saved for aye.
Song of songs, the sto - ry,
Song of glo - ry,

The great assurance of eternal security in Christ is proclaimed in this song written by Howard Jones and Lance Latham.

Mr. Nicholson asked me to join his evangelistic party and play for his meetings. I thought that I could do this and at the same time continue to tutor in mathematics." The mathematics tutoring quickly became impossible, for Lance Latham had committed himself to a course that was to consume the balance of his life on earth. "Decision determines destiny," and so it was with this step in Lance's life.

The first series of meetings for Nicholson's expanded evangelistic team was in the small mining town of Lehighton, Pennsylvania. Once again an auditorium was rented and fliers distributed across the area. People were invited to come and hear the Irish evangelist and the keyboard virtuoso who would lend new sparkle to the music of the crusade. Again, in answer to prayer, people crowded in from every direction and the Spirit of God moved upon the hearts of the lost and needy multitudes from that industrial town.

The Spirit of God was also moving on the platform. Anyone who cared to look would have noticed the pianist of the team listening with rapt attention to the speaker. Night after night the heart of Lance Latham was captured in its attention to the preaching of William P. Nicholson. The scholar-musician was again analyzing the words, but at the same time, a new thing was taking place in his heart. Nicholson emphasized again and again the imperative text from the words of Jesus Christ, "Ye must be born again." That voice echoed across the auditorium, "You may be smart or stupid, you may be rich or poor, you may be black, you may be white, you may be the town drunkard or you may be the mayor; but whoever you are, *you must be born again!*"These words, given life by the Holy Spirit, made their unforgettable impact upon the heart of every listener. Lance himself recalls those days, saying, "It was the same preacher, many of the same sermons, but blessed conviction laid hold of me." This young eastern prodigy became the object of the working of the Holy Spirit. Lance concentrated his mind and heart on the Word of God. The result was the most dramatic moment in the life of any person, the moment of his conversion to Christ.

Following the meeting, Lance knelt in his hotel room and wept before the Lord. When we remember his background, we can understand the difficulties through which he came to the place of faith in the Savior. Writing of this moment, Lance said, "Somehow I seemed to remember only one text ... 'Ye must be born again.' I knew I was lost. Every evening I would go to bed with one thought, 'if you die, you will go to hell forever.' I thought of little else."

Then came the moment of all moments. Lance recalls, "Finally on the afternoon of Friday, September 18, 1915, I knelt in my bedroom in the hotel in which we were staying and I said, 'Lord, I am the sinner who needs You.' I saw the merit of Calvary, not too clearly at first, but I was saved! Salvation is an amazing thing." He rose from his knees on that blessed day, knowing that Jesus Christ had come to live within his life. The Christ of Calvary had become his personal Savior. So began a life, lived for Jesus Christ, that was to accomplish the purpose of Him who works all things after the counsel of His own will.

Lance recalls that he immediately saw the contrast between new life in Jesus Christ and the religious form of the old days. In telling of his conversion, Lance said, "While I was in college, Father would ask, 'Do you read your Bible?' I would lie and say, 'Yes,' partly not to hurt my father's feelings and incidentally not desiring to have mine hurt. I never opened my Bible in college days; neither, as far as I can see, did anyone else. But after being saved, immediately I had a great hunger for the Word of God and a desire to win others to Christ." From

35

that moment on, the life of Lance Latham was a marvelous proof of the truth of the Scripture which says, "If any man be in Christ, he is a new creature; old things are passed away; behold, all things are become new" (II Corinthians 5:17).

Lance took the time to give us his own analysis of the blessed scenario of those days, the events which brought him to the place of faith in Christ. He writes, "William P. Nicholson, a true man of God, came to my hometown of Chester, Pennsylvania for an evangelistic campaign. My father backed up the meetings to the limits. This was not the 'annual revival' limited to a Wednesday through Sunday meeting. No, they meant business for the Lord. It was to be for six weeks, every night but Saturday, for seven Sundays. I remember it turned out to be a ten-week meeting. Hundreds were saved. Father received 234 new members into his Presbyterian church. Not only so, but 279 of the church members were saved. And we had PREACHING. Teaching is also a gift of the Holy Spirit, but preaching is something else. Although both are based on the Word of God, preaching convicts, stirs, and persuades. We are not to be satisfied with teaching only. It took preaching to reach me. Preaching hell, the unpardonable sin, judgment to come; these are subjects which are avoided today, but they need to be preached! William P. Nicholson had the gift."

So it was that in William P. Nicholson, Lance received not only the message of salvation but the illustration of the kind of evangelism in which he would never cease to believe. For all of life, from that moment on, Lance would never be satisfied with anything less than powerful preaching, biblical exposition, and a "no-nonsense" invitation to believe in Christ.

From Lance's statement, we can also discover the answer to an implied question, "Why had not Lance Latham received Christ earlier in life?" His answer to the question is, "It took preaching to reach me." The mind of Lance Latham was unquestionably filled with facts about the Bible and he was an obvious expert on orthodox Christianity. This gradual buildup of knowledge, however, had never brought him to the place of conviction and conversion to Christ. His decision for the Savior clearly demonstrates what the Scripture has already said, *"The preaching of the cross* is to them that perish foolishness; but unto us which are saved it is the power of God" (I Corinthians 1:18).

What a lesson for our time! We know full well that the Bible teaches that "It pleased God by the foolishness of preaching to save them that believe" (I Corinthians 1:21). Nevertheless, our programs foolishly take the form of many other methods which have long shown themselves to be too expensive, unworkable, and unproductive of spiritual results. For all of his life, Lance would insist that the purpose of the Church is to preach and teach the Word of God. The purpose of camping and Awana Clubs is to preach the Word to young people. Nothing amounts to anything if it does not make possible the preaching of the Word. Preaching produces true conversion to Jesus Christ, the kind that lasts.

From the moment of his conversion, Lance was also acutely aware of the difference between religion and real life in Jesus Christ. He would never cease to be concerned for people who had a religious background, who were knowledgeable about the Bible, but who had never been born again. Lance was fond of saying, "In my early years, I read and memorized the Bible but never saw that I myself needed to be saved." He was grateful beyond words for the grace of God that brought him to see his sinful condition and his need of a Savior. From that moment on the word "grace" would be the touchstone of his ministry.

Few have ever been long under the ministry of Lance

Latham who have not frequently sung and memorized the immortal words of John Newton, Lance Latham's favorite hymn.

Amazing grace! how sweet the sound
That saved a wretch like me!
I once was lost, but now am found,
Was blind, but now I see.

'Twas grace that taught my heart to fear,
And grace my fears relieved;
How precious did that grace appear
The hour I first believed!

Thru many dangers, toils and snares,
I have already come;
'Tis grace hath brought me safe thus far,
And grace will lead me home.

When we've been there ten thousand years,
Bright shining as the sun,
We've no less days to sing God's praise
Than when we first begun.

What if William P. Nicholson had not come to Chester, Pennsylvania? The answer may be that the world of music would have given fame and fortune to a concert pianist by the name of Lance Latham. We know, however, that this was not to be. Lance Latham rather brought spirit, soul, and body — he brought all to the foot of the cross of Jesus Christ. The Philadelphia musician became captive to the One who gave His life on Calvary that we all might live.

4

The Truth of the Gospel

"If you are going to be saved, you must surrender all!"

"The gospel is laying down your life for the healing of the nations."

"Faith is where it starts, but only members of this church, the Community of the Spirit, are saved."

"How confusing," thought Lance Latham as he listened to these and other statements in his early visits to churches. "There seems to be a different gospel and a different way of salvation with every preacher I hear." This young and earnest Christian, listening to a sermon on Sunday morning in a local church, became increasingly perplexed. The preacher said many interesting things from the Bible and then took the time to explain the way of salvation. "In order to be a Christian," the preacher said, "you must be totally dedicated to the Lord. You must forsake all or you cannot be saved."

Lance Latham listened to these words with increasing confusion of mind. He remembered that marvelous moment on September 18, 1915, in which Jesus Christ came to live in his life. He was sure that up until that time he had done his best to be committed, moral, and earnest about his religious life. Was salvation then by commitment? By dedication? By hard work? By abandonment to the Lord? The careful mind of Lance

39

Latham simply could not settle for these messages which contradicted so totally the salvation which he knew he had by the grace of God.

Bowing his head in prayer that morning, Lance said, "Dear Lord, teach me, show me, help me to understand." He vowed that he would not rest until he thoroughly understood the basis of salvation. He would give himself to no other pursuit until he truly knew what the Bible said about how a person is saved and has the assurance of everlasting life.

He wrote about that pursuit, "In the course of hearing many preachers, reading Christian books and magazines, I had become utterly bewildered. Was salvation really a free gift? Or must we pay for it by a certain amount of devotion — some outward manifestation, like raising my hand in a meeting, coming forward, joining a church, giving liberally, 'putting my all on the altar'?

"I heard as I traveled around, many different invitations: 'Give your heart to God,' 'Give your life to God,' 'Ask Jesus into your heart,' 'Pray the publican's prayer,' 'Make Jesus Lord of your life,' 'Surrender all to Him.' "

These confusing messages and invitations began for Lance a pursuit of truth which was to make him a most exacting minister of the Word in later life. He recounts this searching at that time, saying, "Although I was truly saved and active in seeking to reach others for Christ, I was yet to make my greatest Bible discovery — *the gospel of the grace of God.*"

No one will understand Latham who does not appreciate the agony of soul which he faced in the process of arriving at his settled conviction as to what was truly the gospel and what is meant by the grace of God. In that day, the Lord was raising up men who were incisive preachers of the Word of God. Latham had the opportunity to hear some of them. He recalls, "Then I heard quite a different line of preaching ... that the work had been fully done on the cross of Calvary and that the price of sin had been fully paid. All I had to do, once I realized my need, was to believe on the Lord Jesus Christ, to believe that He was truly the Son of God, and to put my faith in the finished work of Calvary. I began to see that these messages were very contradictory. Could they both be right?"

So the mind of Lance Latham was torn between a gospel which promised salvation on the basis of human works and one which invited a person to rest in Christ's finished work on the cross, and be saved by grace. The mind of Lance Latham, the musician, mathematician and scholar could not embrace these two views at the same time. He began to see that a gospel of human works was no gospel at all. His conviction grew that the message of salvation by grace alone was the way to eternal life.

Remembering those days, Lance wrote, "During the first six months of my being saved, I came across a well-known tract by Alexander Marshall, 'God's Way of Salvation.' I read a paragraph, 'If I do my part, God will do His. But Scripture nowhere speaks of your part. Your part is simply believing that you are a hell-deserving sinner, and that you can do nothing to save yourself. All you can do is look to what has been done on the cross of Calvary and find your hope in what Christ did for you there.' "

What was Lance's initial reaction? He tore up the booklet! As yet the mind of Lance Latham could not get away from the "religious influences" of the old days. He stared at the pieces on the floor before him, still resenting the presumption that one needs to do nothing whatsoever, but only to believe, to be accepted by God.

But the work of the Holy Spirit in enlightenment was to continue in his life. He writes, "One year later it occurred to me that this tract which I had torn up the year before, saying to myself, 'That is nonsense — you've got to at least be pretty good to stay saved' — this same tract might be right after all. Reading my Bible day by day, I was on my way to solving the greatest perplexity I had ever had. Was salvation really after all a free gift?"

"The greatest perplexity I ever had." It is the rare twenty-one-year-old young man for whom life's greatest perplexity is not a girl friend, an hourly wage, or the kind of car to buy. Not for Lance Latham! All was irrelevant until he finally discovered the answer to the question, "Was salvation after all a free gift?"

He continues to recall the pursuit of those days. "Summertime had come, there were no meetings, and I had the whole summer to myself. I determined to spend every morning reading the Bible and books and magazines that dealt with Bible subjects. I would at least settle 'What is the gospel?' A short while before this, I told a man who wanted to be saved, 'Until you are willing to go to Borneo or wherever God leads you, you will not be saved.' Did I tell him the gospel?"

The burning question now settled upon the mind of Lance Latham that he recalls with conviction to this day, "Did I tell him the gospel?"

We see the picture of a young man poring over the pages of his Bible, thirsting for spiritual truth, for the meaning of salvation. Latham recalls the emotion of those days, saying, "A short time later, I read the awful warning in Galatians 1:8, 'Though we, or an angel from heaven, preach any other gospel unto you than that which we have preached unto you, let him be accursed.' This added terror to my many anxieties. I must find out 'What is the gospel?' "

Out of this confusion of mind and spirit came the great conviction and great discovery for young Lance.

"The more I read the books and Christian magazines, the more perplexed I became. Here was a very fine article in one magazine by Ironside, as true to the Word of God as Dr. Ironside always was. In another column was an article by the editor of the magazine, which just increased my confusion. After about a month of reading everything, I came to a wise conclusion — read the Bible only!

"Now I had, as a boy of seventeen, recited the entire book of Romans, and doubtless had read and reread Romans 3 and 4 many times, but I had never discovered the amazing truth of those chapters. Suddenly one morning I read Romans 3:21, 'BUT NOW THE RIGHTEOUSNESS OF GOD WITHOUT THE LAW IS MANIFESTED.'

"The light of the gospel of grace just flooded my soul!

" 'WITHOUT THE LAW' solved the problem. It was really as Dr. William Pettingill so often expressed it, 'Saved by grace through faith, plus nothing.' "

This discovery was, for Lance Latham, the moment of spiritual ecstasy that established the biblical basis of his message for all of his life. He says, "You can imagine the delight that filled my soul as I continued to read the amazing passage containing such verses as 'Being justified freely by his grace through the redemption that is in Christ Jesus.' 'Through faith in his blood.'

" 'Therefore we conclude that a man is justified by faith without the deeds of the law.' Proceeding to the next chapter, 'But to him that worketh not, but believeth on him that justifieth the ungodly, his faith is counted for righteousness.' No wonder Martin Luther called Romans 3:19 through 4:8 the core of the Epistle to the Romans and said that Romans was the light of the whole Scripture."

Here, Lance Latham, the new Christian, settled the greatest question in all of life, "What is the gospel, the basis of salvation?" In his testimony as to the influence of this moment he recounts, "This was the amazing discovery that has been the heart of my ministry."

Lance Latham once said, "There are three men who have most greatly influenced my ministry and all of them are named Paul." The first one named Paul was of course the Apostle Paul. By reading Paul's Epistle to the Romans, the mind of Lance Latham touched the mind of the great Apostle to the Gentiles. To know Christ as his Savior gave Lance Latham eternal life. To understand the gospel of the grace of God explained by the Apostle Paul in Romans 3 and 4 gave Lance Latham the message and the motivation that was to carry him untiringly through all of life. The gospel of the grace of God became the heart of his ministry. Never again, not once for the rest of his life would Lance ever advise a seeking soul to surrender all to be saved. To preach another gospel was the deepest possible treachery against God. To offer the message of salvation by works was to put the cross of Calvary to shame. From this moment on, Lance would never preach another gospel and also would be instant in his discernment in announcing the issue of perversions of the gospel. When we lose the gospel, all is lost. For Lance, the first Paul in his life is the Apostle Paul, and the message that must always be first and foremost — the gospel of the grace of God!

Nothing has more characterized the ministry of Lance Latham than his concern for the truth of the gospel. No more urgent prayer could be lifted in our time than that this generation might rediscover also the truth of the gospel of the grace of God. Christians are allowed to have many and varied opinions about other subjects in the Word of God. We are, however, allowed no such variation about the exact definition of the gospel. The gospel is that by which we are saved, it is the power of God unto salvation. Carefully defined by the Apostle

Paul, the gospel is the message that "Christ died for our sins according to the Scriptures." To deviate from that truth to the slightest degree brings the terrible judgment of God upon any life and ministry. Who can but weep, therefore, at the hideous versions of the Christian faith which are preached from pulpits, printed in magazines, and proclaimed over radio and television? Without doubt, the central confusion of our time is the fact that, even in what professes to be evangelical Christianity, there are a hundred contradictory answers to the question, "What must I do to be saved?" A new generation which simply does not comprehend the message of justification by faith alone has come into positions of influence and leadership. Speaking from ignorance or perfidy, pulpiteers and promoters are once again subverting the Christian faith by preaching absurdities to which they attach the blessed name "gospel." So it is that many today, ignoring or resenting the work of Calvary, have become enemies of the cross of Christ. Their end is destruction.

Lance Latham made no such mistake. The first passion of his Christian life was to understand and settle from the Word of God alone the truth of the gospel. We who have known him testify that he has never deviated from that sacred message.

Something of that deep and changeless conviction in the life of Lance Latham was recently illustrated to me again. Lance Latham and I, along with Bob Swanson and others, took part in the funeral service for Ole Rorheim, the father of Art Rorheim. The committal service at the cemetery brought a most moving moment when we all sang together an old hymn of the faith. I was standing with Lance, looking into that aged, youthful face. We sang,

"The soul that on Jesus hath leaned for repose,
I will not, I will not desert to his foes;

That soul, though all hell should endeavor to shake,
   I'll never, no, never, no, never forsake!"

Amen! All hell will never shake the soul that believes in the truth of the gospel of the finished work of Calvary's cross. One who believes any other "gospel" will soon be blown about, dislocated, defeated by the new winds of doctrine which are blowing in our time.

Lance's conviction as to the truth of the gospel has been translated into the lives of many others. His preaching through the years was characterized by a repeated emphasis on "the truth of the gospel." The result has been that those who committed their lives to Christian service under Lance's teaching brought with them the same convictions to their ministry and were instantly and easily able to detect error in pulpits and periodicals.

Blessed Calvary!

Avis B. Christiansen, 1895-

Lance B. Latham, 1894-

1. I look at the cross up-on Cal - va - ry, And O what a
won-der di - vine! To think of the wealth it holds for me —
The rich - es of heav - en are mine.

2. I find at the cross bless-ed vic - to - ry, And grace for each
step of the way; The fount of God's love is flow - ing free,
And sweet-er it grows day by day.

3. The cross is my hope for e - ter - ni - ty— No mer - it have
I of my own; The shed blood of Christ my on - ly plea —
My trust is in Je - sus a - lone.

CHORUS

Bless-ed Cal - va - ry! Pre-cious Cal - va - ry! 'Neath thy shad-ow I'll ev - er a - bide; Bless-ed Cal - va - ry! Pre-cious Cal - va - ry! 'Twas there Je-sus suf-fered and died.

Only Jesus

Avis B. Christiansen

Lance B. Latham

1. I've found a ref-uge from life's care in Je-sus, I am
2. I've found a pre-cious joy in know-ing Je-sus, Nev-er
3. I've found a bless-ed hope di-vine in Je-sus, 'Tis a

hid-ing in His love di-vine; He ful-ly un-der-stands my
dreamed of in this world of woe; No clouds, how-ev-er dark, can
Day Star ev-er shin-ing bright; It fills my earth-ly way with

soul's deep long-ing, And He whis-pers soft-ly, "Thou art mine."
dim the ra-diance Of the heav'n-ly light He doth be-stow.
heav'n-ly glo-ry, And it turns life's dark-ness in-to light.

REFRAIN

On-ly Je-sus! On-ly Je-sus! On-ly He can sat-is-fy;

Ev-'ry bur-den be-comes a bless-ing, When I know my Lord is nigh.

5

The Message for Christians

"Mr. Latham, may I please speak to you?"

The evening had been a glorious one with several thousand people attending the great evangelistic service. Once again the preaching reached out to the hearts of people and scores responded to the invitation to receive Christ. Lance played through the verses of the invitation song and then for several minutes afterwards while the crowd was slowly leaving the auditorium. He never failed at this moment to breathe a prayer that God would continue to work in the hearts of people. He prayed, "Dear Lord, help these people to so believe the truth that it will stay with them long after this evening's meeting has been forgotten." Just then he felt a hand on his arm. With shining, earnest eyes, the young man looked into the face of Lance Latham and asked him once again, "Mr. Latham, may I please speak to you?"

Always willing to help, Lance instantly consented to answer whatever question this young seeker would press upon him. The question was a simple one. The lad said, "Mr. Latham, I am a Christian but I want to know, how shall I live my life for Christ?"

These words struck deeply into the heart of Lance Latham and triggered a second spiritual quest that was to lead Lance to his deepest conviction about the strength by which a Christian lives his life for the Lord.

Lance was sure that he had been saved by faith in Jesus Christ, but he now faced the question of the sustaining power of the gospel in the life of the believer. Young people were coming to him, pressed by the need for advice and help in their Christian lives. Lance, out of great concern and love, studied and prayed that God would lead him to an understanding of how the justification of God applied in the lives of those who had believed in Christ. So marvelous was his new realization of the answer to this question that he calls it another discovery. "I had to find the answer to the questions that were pressed upon me by Christians and this led me to another discovery. 'What is the message to those who are saved?' "

"At that time I discovered with joy the book by William Reid, *The Blood of Jesus,* and he says, 'TO BE JUSTIFIED ON THE GROUNDS OF THE SHED BLOOD OF CHRIST PLUS A PRELIMINARY WORK OF REFORMATION OR SUBSEQUENT WORK OF SANCTIFICATION, THE NATURAL MAN CAN EASILY APPROVE OF: BUT TO BE JUSTIFIED ON THE GROUNDS OF THE SHED BLOOD OF CHRIST AND THAT ALONE, IS TOTALLY BEYOND HIS COMPREHENSION.'

"William C. Mackay suggests the same in his wonderful book, *Grace and Truth,* that until you cease from your carnal agility and self-rating activity and consent to be justified by the shed blood of Christ alone, you will never be saved."

That vital second discovery for Lance Latham was the realization that grace is not only the way of salvation, but it is also the key to the sustaining and successful Christian life. All things that come into the life of a Christian are his by the grace of God. Even in those days, much was being said about the work of the Spirit in the life of a believer. This became the object of Lance's concern. He says, "I read much about the fullness of the Spirit. One writer would affirm that if we clean up our past, surrender all, and promise perfect obedience from now on, God would fill us with the Spirit." In the light of the popularity of this message today, Latham's concern for this false doctrine is worth examining.

Lance says, "If this is the case, what did Paul mean when he said in Romans 6:14, 'Sin shall not have dominion over you: for ye are not under the law, but under grace'? What did Paul mean in Galatians 2:21, 'If righteousness come by the law (meaning here 'righteous living'), then Christ is dead in vain'? What about Galatians 3:1-3, 'O foolish Galatians, who hath bewitched you, that ye should not obey the truth, before whose eyes Jesus Christ hath been evidently set forth, crucified among you? This only would I learn of you, Received ye the Spirit by the works of the law, or by the hearing of faith? Are ye so foolish? Having begun in the Spirit, are ye now made perfect by the flesh?'

"Then I thought of Acts 20:32 where Paul says to the Ephesian elders, 'And now, brethren, I commend you to God, and to the *word of his grace*, which is able to build you up.'

"And I thought of Romans 1:16, 'For I am not ashamed of the gospel of Christ; for it is the power of God unto salvation.' (Not merely justification, but our living as well.) Is the entrance into salvation by faith, but the entrance into the fullness of the Spirit by the works of the law? The little word 'for' in the middle of Romans 6:14 intrigued me. I believe both parts of that verse. But why the word 'for'? The answer to my question began to appear; *for the Christian, being under grace brings about what all his legal efforts could never obtain.* It then became all-important to discover what it means to be 'under grace.'"

Lance continues, "The answer is in many of the

Epistles, especially those of Paul. The answer is discovering that I have everything in Christ, believing it, and resting in it. Chapters such as Romans 5-8, Ephesians 1-3, Colossians 1 and many other passages began to open for me the marvelous panorama of grace — I have everything in Christ. Where is the path unto the fullness of God? I find one passage that is the sure answer. It is in Paul's prayer in Ephesians 3:16-21. This is God's key to the fullness of Christ.

> That he would grant you, according to the riches of his glory, to be strengthened with might by his Spirit in the inner man; that Christ may dwell in your hearts by faith; that ye, being rooted and grounded in love, may be able to comprehend with all saints what is the breadth, and length, and depth, and height; and to know the love of Christ, which passeth knowledge, that ye might be filled with all the fulness of God. Now unto him that is able to do exceeding abundantly above all that we ask or think, according to the power that worketh in us, unto him be glory in the church by Christ Jesus throughout all ages, world without end. Amen.

"Here are two of the most wonderful prayers in the Bible: the first is in Ephesians 1:15-23 and the second is here in the third chapter. In the first chapter, God would open our eyes to what we have in Christ.

> Wherefore I also, after I heard of your faith in the Lord Jesus, and love unto all the saints, cease not to give thanks for you, making mention of you in my prayers; that the God of our Lord Jesus Christ, the Father of glory, may give unto you the spirit of wisdom and revelation in the knowledge of him: the eyes of your understanding being enlightened; that ye may know what is the hope of his calling, and what the riches of the glory of his inheritance in the saints, and what is the exceeding greatness of his power to usward who believe, according to the working of his mighty power, which he wrought in Christ, when he raised him from the dead, and set him at his own right hand in the heavenly

places, far above all principality, and power, and might, and dominion, and every name that is named, not only in this world, but also in that which is to come; and hath put all things under his feet, and gave him to be the head over all things to the church, which is his body, the fulness of him that filleth all in all.

"In this prayer, Paul is asking God to give the Ephesians the spirit of wisdom and revelation in the knowledge of Him. In the third chapter, Paul is asking God that they might be strengthened in the inner man. This is not obtained by self-sacrifice, vows, resolutions or intense efforts, but is part of His amazing gift through Christ. This is their possession always. 'For in him dwelleth all the fullness of the Godhead bodily;' and they are 'complete in him.' In chapter one we find the word 'give' is used; in chapter three it is 'grant' — this is all of grace. How wonderfully it harmonizes with Ephesians 1:3 where we are told that God has blessed us with all spiritual blessings in Christ."

We must never believe that these convictions which came from the Word of God to the heart of Lance Latham were merely abstract doctrines that had no relevance to life. We shall see that these convictions made his a life that influenced thousands and then, through them, millions of others across the world. The marvelous ministry that was to follow grew out of the great joy that came to the heart of this young seeker after truth because of the two discoveries he made from the Word of God — grace for salvation and grace for living.

Concerning God's grace, Lance writes, "Knowing the love of God as well as His other mercies, is God's powerful motivation to encourage us to present our bodies a living sacrifice.

"To present Romans 12:1 as a *command* is utterly wrong. It can be very legal. Paul *beseeches* with the powerful encouragement of the 'mercies of God,' which will bring about a submissive heart. Vows offered cannot obtain this. Even if they could, the sacrifice would not be acceptable to God. 'Though I bestow all my goods to feed the poor, and though I give my body to be burned, and have not love, it profiteth me nothing.' "

What produced the powerful motivation in the lives of many others to respond with the investment of their lives as a result of the preaching of Lance Latham? What moved those young people who went by the hundreds into the service of Christ across the world because of the influence of Lance?

We have a clue in his own writing, "How can this powerful motivation of love be produced in our lives? God has already told us, 'The love of God is shed abroad in our hearts by the Holy Ghost which is given unto us.' Here, right in the beginning of Paul's epistle we are told what we have in Christ. This is constantly the basis of so many of Paul's exhortations. In Romans 6, our victory is based on the fact that we have been crucified with Christ and risen with Him. We are to believe God and reckon on this that we have. In Romans 7, we have been delivered from the law."

Lance Latham saw that the Christian life is not earning new credits and blessings from the Lord. Instead, the Christian life is the grateful response to what the Lord has already done for us in that He has given us everything in Christ. No Christian will therefore be effective who sees his life as slavish servitude to legal rules. Rather, he will be motivated to exploits and accomplishments when he sees himself not as serving the law but responding to grace. So it was with the Apostle Paul who said, "By the grace of God I am what I am" (I Corinthians 15:10).

Those of us who have heard Lance Latham preach hundreds of times will recall that he has said to us in many ways such things as "How foolish to seek to earn what we already have. How foolish to try to crucify ourselves. How foolish to seek to produce love by our prayers and efforts when we already have the love of God shed abroad in our hearts. I read one translation which said, 'We are drenched inside with the love of God.'

"God wants us to believe these glorious things. Our life is one step of faith after another. How challenging is the word from the Apostle Paul, 'Fight the good fight of faith.' We naturally think we have the resources; whereas God tells us in ourselves there is no good thing."

Lance Latham was well aware of the work of the Holy Spirit in all of these things. Those who listened to his teaching came to an early biblical understanding of the precious working of this heavenly guest in their personal lives and the life of His Church.

Lance says, "It will be helpful for us as we consider the nature of the working of the Holy Spirit in our own lives to compare what the Apostle Paul says in Ephesians 5:18-19 and his earnest word in Colossians 3:16: 'Be filled with the Spirit; speaking to yourselves in psalms and hymns and spiritual songs, singing and making melody in your heart to the Lord', and 'Let the word of Christ dwell in you richly in all wisdom; teaching and admonishing one another in psalms and hymns and spiritual songs, singing with grace in your hearts to the Lord.'

"We see that in both passages the result is the same — the happy, joyous heart. There is something very much in common therefore between being 'filled with the Spirit' and letting the 'Word of Christ dwell in you richly in all wisdom.'

"The Holy Spirit and the Word of God always go together. The wonderful result of these verses takes place as the Holy Spirit uses the Word of God, not our feeble efforts. 'The Word of God is quick and powerful, sharper than any two-edged sword.' The Spirit of God reminds us of what we have in Christ, of God's choosing us for all eternity, of His love that passes knowledge, of His plans for us through all eternity. Therefore, what the law could not do, grace does wonderfully. How wonderful it is not to be under the law but under grace! 'The law made nothing perfect, but the bringing in of a better hope did' (Hebrews 7:19)."

Again and again Lance would extend a call to personal holiness on the part of those who heard him. He was convinced that a testimony for Christ must be backed up with a godly life, and he illustrated this in every one of his actions. Every person who knew him during his long and fruitful ministry would testify that he was one of the most godly men whom they had ever met. He was instant in prayer, moved with compassion for others, and careful to maintain a life that was rich in good works. He continued to insist that the gospel of the grace of God results in a godly life. Again and again he emphasized the way of forgiveness and cleansing to Christians. I John 1:9 gives us God's answer. 'If we confess our sins, he is faithful and just to forgive us our sins, and to cleanse us from all unrighteousness.' "

One who heard Lance over the years remembers, "Lance always brought out the fact that victory in one's life was obtained in much the same manner as salvation. 1. Believe, receive, accept — regarding Calvary for salvation. 2. Reckon yourself dead unto sin, but alive unto God. How? In the same way — by appropriating, receiving, believing — not by works."

Grace is the answer. This deepest of all convictions settled upon the heart of Lance Latham within a year after his conversion to Christ. He *knew* with unshakeable faith that he had now discovered the message that could answer every need of a thirsty and lost world. The message was grace — grace for salvation, and grace for living.

The preaching of the gospel of grace has been questioned by legalists in all of the history of the church. "People must be made to live in fear of the law," they insist, "or they'll never produce anything that really matters in their lives. Grace produces neglect, whereas obligation can only come to pass with a little law thrown in."

The story of the ministry that has become the lengthened shadow of Lance B. Latham would certainly refute this assertion. The Apostle James has reminded us that "faith without works is dead." It seems, however, that the people who need to be least reminded of that admonition are those whose lives are lived in a grateful response to that marvelous message of grace. In the course of his sixty years of faithful ministry, Lance Latham reminded many an audience that "the grace of God that bringeth salvation hath appeared to all men, teaching us that, denying ungodliness and worldly lusts, we should live soberly, righteously, and godly, in this present world." The results, apparent in the lives of those who have been touched by his lifetime of ministry, are abundant proof of this.

From the golden days at Chicago Gospel Tabernacle came many men who have gone on to significant accomplishment. Evangelist Charles Fuller was touched by the ministry of Paul Rader. Torrey Johnson was moved by the preaching of those days and went on to found Youth For Christ. From out of the old Tab came Ray Schulenberg, one of the original founders of Youth For Christ in the Chicago and Illinois area. Chief White Feather (Tayet Ramar) was a part of those days. He appeared before Queen Mary of England and sang for her "I'd Rather Have Jesus".

Clarence and Howard Jones were touched by the

57

gospel in that era, Howard moving on to a great ministry in Milwaukee, working together with George Ziemer at the Wisconsin Tabernacle. Clarence, as we all know, founded Radio Station HCJB in Quito, Ecuador, reaching the world for Christ.

Peter Deyneka was touched with the gospel through the preaching of Paul Rader at the old Moody Tabernacle. Today the Slavic Gospel Association, founded by this exiled Russian, touches our generation for Christ. Paul Fleming was there, and the result was New Tribes Mission. Howard Ferrin went from the Tabernacle to found Providence Bible Institute, now known as Barrington College. In the Tabernacle days, Lance Latham saw the ministry of Paul Rader send many out to reach the world.

In the ministry of the North Side Gospel Center, the effect of the preaching of the grace of God was the same. Elaine Mielke ministered in Mexico, then married Cameron Townsend, president of Wycliffe Bible Translators. Harry Saulnier, associated with Lance at the Center, founded the world's best-known rescue mission, Pacific Garden Mission in Chicago. Victor Cory came out of the Center and organized Scripture Press, producing Sunday School materials for thousands of churches in America. Howard Hawkinson helped organize Friday night Bible classes at the Tabernacle and became one of the founding fathers of the Center. His daughter Carol married Richard Sisson, the second pastor at the Center. Harvey Prost helped found the North Side Gospel Center. His son Gil is now one of Latin America's most distinguished missionary translators, and his daughter Fay and her husband are also missionaries in Bolivia.

Bill Merrifield was taught at the Center; he is active with Wycliffe Translators as Director of Anthropology and the Summer Institute of Linguistics at Norman, Oklahoma. While he and his family served in Mexico, he translated the whole New Testament into the Chinantec language. Bob Barron came from the Center and is now Christian Education director at the Lake Harriet Baptist Church in Minneapolis. Bill Johnson came to Christ at the Center and now pastors the Morraine Valley Baptist Church in Palos Heights, Illinois. Cal Hibbard accepted Christ at the Center and with Cornelia, his wife, has been active for many years on the Wycliffe Bible Translators staff.

Lance Latham would be the first to say, when examining these glorious results, that this was not his doing. He would testify, "This is the Lord's doing and it is marvelous in our eyes."

Lance would insist, "What the world needs to understand is that the gospel of Jesus Christ is not what they think it is. It is not a sweet announcement that God has come into the world to help us fulfill ourselves. It is the story of man's desperate, lost condition, and of the amazing transformation which takes place in his life when he believes in the gift of salvation as an absolutely free gift. If a person has a Christianity that does not consist of grace, he has no Christianity at all. When he does believe that he is saved entirely and solely by the grace of God, he will see results produced in his life that will astonish even himself. People have accomplished infinitely more when they labor for Christ as a glad response to the gospel of the grace of God rather than with the thought of earning something from Him. The Apostle Paul said, 'By the grace of God I am what I am,' and we need to discover in our lives what this means. Grace produces results, whereas law-keeping makes only for frustration. The gospel of the grace of God will liberate the individual into a life of service for Christ and if it were newly understood by the Church today, it would electrify present-day Christianity. The problem of our present time is that it believes a message which is nothing but warmed-over Judaism rather than the liberty that comes from faith in the finished work of Christ on the cross."

So it was that in the heart of Lance Latham, God, through His Word, established a course that was to lead into ever-widening fields of spiritual opportunity. His life became a testimony of grace.

Who can deny that the message of grace is the need of our lost generation? The Church in the world of the 1970s awaits the realization of its greatest potential when it discovers not new methods, but when it rediscovers the message it professes to believe. People will become capable for Christ in their own right, beyond what unctuous admonition will ever produce, when they see themselves as children of God, set free from the bondage of corruption and brought into the glorious liberty of the sons of God, this by understanding His grace.

6

The Second Paul

The strong voice ebbed and flowed across the large, sawdust-aisled auditorium. To many who were in that great meeting, no one had spoken to the city of Chicago like this since the days of D. L. Moody.

The voice came from the cheery, mobile man who stood behind the pulpit. His eyes sparkled as he reached out with voice and heart to the thousands who listened, who laughed, who wept. He was a preacher, communicator, story teller — one of the best in history. He said, "There I was, standing on Wall Street in New York's money center with a telegram held in my trembling hand, facing the greatest challenge that life had ever brought to me. Three little words were typed on the telegram — three little words, one of five letters, the next of three, and the third of four. Yet the question they asked shook me to my soul's boots! They challenged me with all my failures; they showed me up. They challenged all my philosophy of life. They challenged all my accomplishments. They challenged all my plans; they challenged all my future; and out of all this challenging came the revolution that started life's greatest adventure for me. I am telling you of my challenge, that you, too, in some way, may be challenged and that the new revolution may reach you and recruit you also as an adventurer.

Paul Rader, outstanding evangelist and preacher of the
gospel of grace, became the "second Paul" in the life of
Lance Latham.

"But, you must know something about my life before that moment so that you can understand those three little words..." He had the crowd in the palm of his hand as they listened to the story, the life, the preaching of this man, the incomparable Paul Rader. He was speaking to the working men and women of Chicago who were crammed on the long board benches of the old Moody Tabernacle. Something about his preaching made them come back night after night to hear the next message and the next. Night after night, when the invitation was given, hundreds responded to receive Jesus Christ. A high percentage of these men were those who went on to become the backbone of the new and dynamic Christian community in Chicago. Among them were young people who responded to his challenge to "step into life's greatest adventure" and gave their lives to the service of Jesus Christ.

The three little words, by the way, were "Fixed for what?" Paul Rader, when he had landed a good job in New York City, wired his wife to tell her that it seemed as if nothing could stop him from making a small fortune. His wife, who was visiting their two daughters in Tacoma, Washington received the telegram from Paul, "We are fixed for life." The telegram had arrived with a mistake, however, and said, "We are fixed for like." Her return wire was simply the curious question, "Fixed for what?" These were the three words in the form of a curious telegram from his wife that shocked Paul Rader into realizing that life was not made of business success. The result was that he gave himself to the service of Christ, and by this time had been invited to become the pastor of Chicago's Moody Tabernacle. Paul Rader was also president of the Christian and Missionary Alliance and preached with a great heart about salvation from sin and the need of the world. Many were there who would be affected by his ministry.

Peter Deyneka was there. He had just come from his Russian homeland all the way to Chicago where he had received Christ. Paul Rader was to inspire him to begin a mission to reach the Slavic people of the world. Since those days, the Slavic Gospel Association has become a mighty instrument in the hands of God.

Clarence Jones was there. From the impact of Paul Rader's ministry, God was to lead this young man out to South America to found the great Christian radio station HCJB in Quito, Ecuador. HCJB now produces a signal that reaches around the world with the message of life.

The names of future Christian leaders who were touched by the message of Paul Rader in those days would fill a very large page. Few who were there will ever forget the dramatic moving of the Spirit of God upon the city of Chicago and the ministry of Paul Rader.

Paul Rader's Chicago in 1918 and into the 1920s was a blustering, burgeoning city. It was the city of Al Capone, of prohibition wars, of the Untouchables. It was the city that no evangelist could shut down. But Paul Rader touched Chicago as few men have, before or since.

Into the Chicago of 1918 arrived the young man from Chester, Pennsylvania, Lance Latham. This trip was to deeply intertwine his life with Paul Rader, with Chicago, with tens of thousands of Chicago's toiling masses who, because of that ministry, were to come to Jesus Christ.

Lance came to Chicago for a primary purpose, to attend the Moody Bible Institute. "Lance, you need training in the Bible or you never will be effective for God." These words of a friend in Chester crystallized the feeling within him that he must become an expert in the Scriptures in order to be an effective servant of the Lord. The young concert pianist for whom music was once a full life, had now turned the corner. A new primary had taken over in his life — the Scriptures and the teaching of the Word of God. Yes, music would always be important, but he must give himself to the one activity that could truly alter the lives of people. He must be an expositor of Scripture so that others could understand the gospel of the grace of God. So it was that Lance found himself that fall day in 1918 on the corner of Chicago Avenue and LaSalle Street. He was there to attend "the school that D. L. Moody founded."

"How do you do. My name is Howard Ferrin." So a young man introduced himself to Lance. This meeting at Moody Bible Institute was the beginning of a lifelong friendship.

"Lance was soon the amazement of all the students," reports Howard Ferrin. His ability at the keyboard was discovered and he inevitably was invited to be the pianist for most of the student activities. Quickly this led to invitations to the nearby churches of Chicago and instant recognition on the part of pastors and people that no ordinary musician had come onto the Chicago scene. Above all else, however, Lance looked forward to the opportunity of hearing the famous minister at the Moody Tabernacle just up LaSalle Street, a few blocks from the Institute. Hearing Paul Rader was another step on the path of destiny in the life of Lance Latham. Paul Rader became the second Paul in Latham's life.

The congregation stood to sing "I Love to Tell the Story." As the Tabernacle echoed with enthusiastic voices, Paul Rader came to the platform, aware that the piano accompaniment was something different, someone new. He turned to see the slight figure and aquiline face at the keyboard. He listened with careful attention to the solo that this Moody student played that evening. Following the service it happened again. As had William P. Nicholson in days gone by, Paul Rader now said, "Young man, you must come to Moody Tabernacle and be on our musical staff. A talent like yours must be used for the glory of God. Will you start next week?" The preaching of Paul Rader had already convinced Lance Latham that this man knew the gospel of the grace of God and was one of its most able representatives. The answer he gave was, "Yes, I would be honored to be a part of the music of this great church." So began an association that was to leave its mark upon the life of Lance Latham. It would leave its mark also on the city of Chicago...and the world.

The ministry of Paul Rader at the Moody Tabernacle was a never-to-be-forgotten experience. The emerging spiritual force in the city of Chicago was the evangelistic program of the old Moody Tabernacle. Hundreds had been converted to Christ on Chicago's Near North Side under the ministry of Eli Willi. In 1915, the congregation found itself without a pastor. They heard of the ministry of a young evangelist named Paul Rader, then associated with the Christian and Missionary Alliance. They wondered about the possibility that his burning energy and spiritual intensity might be focused on this most difficult place, Chicago's Near North Side. Paul Rader was invited to Chicago and a capacity house gathered to hear this unusual evangelist of the gospel of the grace of God.

The first meeting was a stunning one. Paul spoke candidly, even critically to the people, chiding them for their traditionalism and their archaic allegiance to men of other days. He reminded them that now was the time for the major thrust in Chicago. He painted a gripping picture of the dying multitudes of Chicago and the world to that audience. He then preached sin and righteousness and judgment under the conviction and blessing of the Holy Spirit.

Some might call it hypnosis, but every Christian knew it was the Lord. They were sure that the Spirit of the Lord Himself had moved among them in a special way in that meeting. Paul Rader was invited to become pastor of Moody Church by acclamation of a congregation that was sure that this would be the dawn of a new era.

And indeed it was. Week after week, people came by the thousands to listen to the man for whom knowing Jesus Christ was the greatest adventure in all of life. Few today can imagine the immense impact that came to the hearts and lives of those who heard "P. R.," as he was affectionately called. They could not get enough of him; their hearts were lifted from discouragement under his gracious ministry. He invited Chicago to the glorious hope of Jesus Christ. Enthusiasm for the gospel and the adventure of living for Christ mounted like a tide in Chicago under the ministry of Paul Rader. So amazing was the impact of this early Chicago evangelist that we do well to note who he was from a spiritual point of view.

In his book, *Life's Greatest Adventure,* Paul Rader describes something of his early life. "I had come away from my college training without the God of the Bible, and without a Bible, a modernly educated so-called Christian, a spiritual wanderer, a speculator groping in the modern darkness that has come upon the world. I came to college a mere boy, all aglow to be a young preacher. I had a father who was a Methodist preacher, a grandfather who was a Methodist preacher, and a great-grandfather who was also a Methodist preacher; and I myself was 'vaccinated' for it! But college, with its 'doubt' propaganda and daily preachments of materialism, negatived every evangelical tendency. Still, some power seemed to be forcing me to go on as a minister."

Rader also tells about the loss of his faith. "I had a father who was a real preacher, who knew God, and who was a man whom God used. He came to see me after I was ordained. Oh, the sadness of it! 'Could I not believe as I used to believe?' How pathetic his face as I answered him, saying that all such beliefs were to me like blocks of

67

ice floating on a river on which I could not step across, because they slipped from under my faith feet and left me floundering in the cold water of freezing doubt!

"I left the ministry of course, for I had no message for men and women. Why should I stand as a preacher, as an under-shepherd, when I had no food for the sheep?"

Paul went on a spiritual search. He later described his impressions as he felt the beginning of spiritual discovery by reading the account of Jesus and Lazarus in John 11. "He cares! He cares! His tears are in His eyes for them out of *pure, marvelous* sympathy! My heart was all aflame. My brain was staggering with the answer to a mighty puzzle. I cried out, 'If You are the Messiah, the Son of God, and if You represent God on this earth, and are crying out of pure sympathy because You care, I'll follow You wherever You may lead while there's a drop of blood left in my body.' "

But Paul Rader still needed to come to the assurance of salvation. He describes this marvelous decision. "I knelt and cried. When I said, 'cleanseth me,' the Spirit of the Living God witnessed within my heart in great assurance and blessing! Oh, the joy of finding cleansing and escape from sin; finding the gift of righteousness, God's righteousness, a perfect life credited to me in place of my sin! *Grace in place of law.*"

So Paul Rader came to understand the gospel of the grace of God. The result was that he became a flaming evangel of the cross of Christ, especially in the city of Chicago.

It was the preaching of Paul Rader that galvanized the careful mind of Lance Latham and brought him into the life and ministry of this man. Lance remembers those days, "I came to Chicago to be a student at Moody Bible Institute. I was there only a short while when I heard of Paul Rader and was invited to the Moody Tabernacle, of which he had been the pastor for some five years. I was quite impressed by the five-thousand-seat auditorium, but I thought I would rather attend a smaller church where I could get to know people and feel at home. Then, after several weeks, I heard Paul Rader again. This time I had quite a different impression. The large auditorium was filled to capacity. What attracted me was a man who had been a prizefighter preaching an hour and a quarter, the last half hour with tears in his eyes as he pleaded with folks to believe on Christ. My mind was made up. But I never had a thought that I would be directly connected with the work."

This was the beginning, and soon the ministry of Lance Latham expanded in the direction that was to characterize his lifetime activity. Lance remembers, "They gave me different jobs to do, and one was having charge of the boys and girls under ten years of age, some hundred of them in Sunday afternoon meetings. Another was the teaching of the Brass Band Sunday School Class. The youngest member was ten-year-old Howard Jones, and Mr. Obertop was over sixty.

"A liberal college education does not fit one for this kind of work. But the constant encouragement of Paul Rader and the wonderful folks at the Moody Church overlooked failures and gave me ability to go on. Then, next, they gave me charge of the special music."

While Lance speaks humbly of these emerging responsibilities, we must remember that these were the days in which Paul Rader, in addition to speaking to five thousand people on Sunday, sometimes preached six nights a week. It would be difficult to think of a comparable ministry which has taken place anywhere on earth on a regular basis since those days. Paul Rader had an electrifying effect upon Chicago in the seven remarkable years during which he ministered at the Moody Tabernacle.

"We must have Paul Rader come to our city!" said

many a pastor and Christian leader across America. Invitations for his preaching ministry poured in from New York, Minneapolis, Los Angeles, and many places in between. Paul Rader read these pleading letters and asked whether God was now leading him to be an evangelist in many places across the world. It soon seemed as if the answer was "Yes!" So the day came when Paul left Moody Tabernacle and began conducting campaigns across America.

Adding an incomparable musical touch to these great crusades was the piano artistry of Lance Latham. This young musician played for some of the largest crowds to gather in the cities of America. In his travels, Latham had the opportunity to see the public and the private Paul Rader. He never failed in his conviction that here was a man of God whom the Lord was using to touch the world.

But then the call came that was almost like that extended by the man from Macedonia. "Come back to Chicago and help us!" Scores of people had gathered to petition Paul Rader to return to Chicago to open a new and greater work. So, Chicago continued to be the city of destiny for Paul Rader...and for Lance Latham.

7

Virginia

"Lance, we must return to Chicago."

Paul Rader spoke to his young musician friend and explained the call that had come from hundreds of concerned people on Chicago's Near North Side. "We have been invited to conduct a crusade in a tabernacle that the committee will build for the occasion." Lance listened to these words with great interest, for the magnetism of Chicago took many forms for him. There was Chicago's spiritual need. There was Paul Rader's own burning heart for Chicago. There was another attraction as well.

Virginia lived in Chicago!

Lance's association with Miss Highfield from Chicago's North Side had begun at the old Moody Tabernacle. Had we been there, we probably would not have noticed the shy, attractive, sixteen-year-old girl who slipped into the back row of the Tabernacle at North Avenue and Clark Street. She would appear to be just another one of the thousands who came from across Chicago, drawn by the magnetism of the preaching of Paul Rader. Little did anyone realize then the major part she was to play in the ministry of the pianist on the platform. Who could have realized that Virginia Highfield, the future Mrs. Lance B. Latham, was in the audience that evening? Who can explain the threads of providence which bring lives together, resulting in new things to the glory of God? Like that of Lance, the story of Virginia Latham is a spiritual saga. We prevailed upon Virginia to put some of this into her own words.

She writes, "I have ever been thankful to the Lord that I was born into a godly home. Although I was not saved until I was sixteen years of age, my early training gave me a start in the right direction. Sunday school, church, and a mother who faithfully taught me all the Bible stories, helped a great deal when I finally received new life in Christ. This happened when I heard the Bible preached by one of God's special servants, Paul Rader. The Word came alive to me."

Virginia's story is similar to that of thousands who were touched by these ministries in the city of Chicago. Chicago, like most of the major metropolitan areas of the world, had no lack of religion. To this very day, churches dot the horizon and preaching comes from behind thousands of pulpits. In the midst of it all, a new fountainhead of spiritual life was rising like a geyser in Chicago, one that was to attract the thirsty from their backgrounds in religion to come to the true fountain of life which is Jesus Christ.

She continues, "I was brought up in a Swedish Covenant Church. It was true to the Word but somehow I really never heard the true gospel there. I heard about sin, hell, heaven, and Calvary, but never did I ever hear that I had no righteousness good enough for God. I was taught to believe Christ died for my sin, but I also thought that I did have quite a bit of righteousness because of my training at home. Then, of course, I was told that the commandments had to be kept in order to keep me saved. I went down the aisle in answer to altar calls each year when the Swedish evangelist came around, and went to ask God to forgive anything that was not good that I had done. I still thought that I reserved a good portion of my own righteousness."

In the midst of it all, Virginia's godly parents

continued to pray for her. Her life parallels that of many, in that parents with spiritual concern did their best to introduce her to true faith, but something else was needed to bring her across the line into the ark of safety. That "something else" is inevitably the forceful preaching of the Word of God.

Virginia remembers her parents' concern, saying, "My dear mother realized that I was not a saved girl and she prayed for me. At one time she said, 'Virginia, you are a good girl, but you are not a saved girl. You do not have eternal life.' This conversation woke me up to my need, and she began to ask me to attend the big meetings which were held at the Moody Tabernacle on Clark and North Avenue where Paul Rader was preaching night after night. The Tabernacle was crowded at every meeting and Mother and Dad loved to go there. There I heard the truth about my own lost condition. I came under deep conviction which constantly bore into me even during high school classes. The Lord was seeking me! I was convinced I needed to be saved. But what would people in our church think of that, for I was teaching a Sunday School class, singing, and even getting up in the young people's meetings with a word about the Lord although I did not know Him! The old sinful nature can act very religious."

Then came that moment of all moments— the moment when religion turns to salvation, the instant when blind eyes see the light of the truth of Jesus Christ, and faith is exercised to the saving of the soul. No Christian ever forgets the day when Christ comes to live within. So it was with Virginia.

She writes, "It was a Sunday night in February, 1917, that I could not go on any longer in refusal of Christ. When I got home from the Sunday night service, I sank to my knees before a chair in my room. With a view of Calvary which Paul Rader had set before us so vividly, I told the Lord I was just a lost sinner and that I believed the way to heaven was through the work of Christ dying for me. It was in nothing that I had ever done or could do. What a relief! A peace flooded my soul. I was standing now on solid ground for the first time in my life."

The message of the gospel preached by Paul Rader had reached another heart, bringing a "religious but lost" person to the foot of the cross. Again the gospel of the grace of God penetrated into the world of religion, pointing up the subtle counterfeit of the practice of "the Christian religion," and the difference between this and faith in the Savior. As was the case with thousands of young people who came under the preaching of the gospel in the city of Chicago, the decision for Christ which Virginia made was to call for some subsequent difficult choices. Her story continues.

"The next thing that faced me at sixteen years of age was that I could not stand the old church any longer. My heart longed to be where God was working, and after facing life's future, I bade my old friends good-bye on a Sunday morning in the old church. I gave up my class, and after Sunday School I walked north on LaSalle Street to the Tabernacle *alone*, with tears coursing down my face. I just *had* to make this decision. Now I know it was the Holy Spirit leading me in His path that 'He had foreordained that I should walk in it.' I was His workmanship and wanted God to use me."

Here Virginia includes a word of admonition to all others who would read her spiritual history. "If you are a young person reading this, may I urge you to leave anything that is not moving for God and get into a church where the true gospel of grace is preached and where there is an outreach to the lost world."

There is an old song that says, "There's a line that we

cross by rejecting the Lord, where the call of the Spirit is lost." This is frighteningly true, as many of the degenerates of our world have discovered. It is also true that there is a line that we cross by accepting the Lord. The person who comes to Jesus Christ begins to walk in the light of the gospel which illuminates his pathway as never before. This sunlight from heaven clearly points up the absurdity of his past life, even his past religious life. So it is that every new Christian realizes that coming to Jesus Christ is not the emotion of a moment, it is the beginning of a new pathway to glory that takes a different direction from the one that he has followed. The spiritual discernment that comes with salvation helps him to see that he must cross a line from the old life to the new and cut clean from the past. Inevitably, faith in Jesus Christ calls us out, not only from the world of sin, but also from the world of religion.

Virginia continues her story. "When I reached the Tabernacle, it was in the midst of the morning service. I crept into a back bench — alone — I did not know anyone. My folks were there and were overjoyed to see me. But although I was alone, I was very happy. I knew I was where God wanted me. At the close of the service, young people gathered around and invited me to the Christian Companionship Club that evening. There I found new friends, and within a week I was in a big choir."

The pianist for that choir and for all other activities at the Tabernacle was, of course, Lance Latham. By this time, everyone at the Moody Tabernacle called him "Doc." No one knows quite where it started, but Doc was his name.

"Virginia, I wonder if you would be willing to help us by singing in a girls' trio we want to form?" The heart of Virginia Highfield leaped at this invitation; unbelievable as it seemed to her, here was another opportunity to

75

serve Christ with her soprano voice. The crowd was delighted at the expanding music program and amazed at the way their young music director, Doc, could organize these many groups. They called for more. "Virginia, would you be willing to sing a solo in the service this next Sunday evening?" Virginia thought, "Is it possible that he is inviting me? Inviting me...to sing a solo in a meeting with Paul Rader?" Again, she listened in unbelief. That glorious moment of opportunity was followed by another. "Virginia, I wonder if I may have the privilege of taking you home after the service tonight?" So it was that the young musician began to suggest the possibility of a personal association with this beautiful soprano soloist who had moved into the circle of his attention. Lance and Virginia began "keeping company" and the folks at the church looked on with a measure of surprise. They had long wondered who might capture the heart of this eligible prodigy at the piano and now they thought that their question might soon be answered. Virginia Highfield and Lance B. Latham; hmmm...perhaps.

Virginia soon discovered that the path of the just is as a shining light. A life that truly decides to take the narrow way in allegiance to Christ is soon moving in the midst of spiritual opportunity. Virginia recounts her story. "One of the greatest privileges I had in those days was singing, often alone, in the evening services before Paul Rader preached to a packed Tabernacle seating five thousand people. How good the Lord has been! Little did I know that I would be married to that pianist some day, and that the two of us would have the sweet ministry the Lord has led us into in the years since then. What memories of a precious walk with the One who died for us!"

One of Virginia Latham's most apparent early gifts was that of music. She sang in the great Tabernacle choir

Lance Latham and Virginia Highfield, heirs together of the grace of life.

Lance and Virginia, October 14, 1924. The wedding was celebrated on a Tuesday to avoid disrupting the Saturday evening meetings for high school young people at the Tabernacle...an indication of priorities that continued to be shown in their lives.

and in smaller groups, one of which was a quartet which included her parents. There was "a certain something" about her solo voice, and its ability to speak through the voice of music to great audiences that listened. She was able to take the grand old hymns as well as the conventional newer solo numbers and sing them into the waiting hearts in many an audience. Many of us who heard her will never forget the special blessing her music was. I am often moved to remember how beautifully she sang,

"Savior, Thy dying love Thou gavest me;
Nor should I aught withhold, dear Lord, from Thee;
In love my soul would bow, my heart fulfill its vow,
Some offering give Thee now, something for Thee."

We can all exactly picture how Lance Latham listened from the piano keyboard to the song of this young, blithe spirit and noted the sweet, spiritual nature from which it was sung. He began to picture this beautiful girl standing by his side for all of his future. He knew that in Virginia Highfield was the intelligence, the talent, and the spiritual dedication that would complement his personality and ministry. Not surprisingly then, the day came in the early 1920s when he asked Virginia to marry him. These two young people chose to become heirs together of the grace of life.

Recalling this, Virginia writes, "Doc has been a wonderful husband. Yes, he heard me sing and I guess I sang into his heart. I hadn't planned it that way. We kept company for two years and we delighted in being in the Lord's service. We read the Bible together and talked of spiritual things constantly. He really took time to get me straightened out about what it means to live under grace as well as being saved by grace. He was a godly boy with real standards and that was what I wanted. Not just any old fellow could get my attention, and all of this was because I really wanted God's will more than anything else. It must be very difficult for a real Christian girl to be married to a carnal Christian whose real interest is not in God's program for him."

The years moved ahead to 1924 at the Chicago Gospel Tabernacle. Virginia writes, "We worked and trusted together. We were married on October 14, 1924 on a Tuesday night because we did not want to break into the important high school meetings for boys and girls which took place every Saturday night at the Tabernacle. Our wedding was unusual although it was never planned to be that way. The Sunday before, Mr. Rader invited everyone to come, so we had a full house — about five thousand people!"

In Virginia Highfield, Lance Latham took to himself a wife who was to be a great strength to him in his ministry, and who was also to have a remarkable ministry of her own in music, youth camps, girls' work, Bible teaching, and a world of other activities. Her spiritual perceptions were always a trustworthy resource to Lance. Often, when he felt he could not even trust his own mind, he rejoiced in the "sanctified intuition" which Virginia supplied in the critical decisions which were to be made in the days to come.

Through the years, invitations came to Virginia from many quarters to conduct Bible classes. In 1943, she was invited by Mrs. Constance Hallworth to conduct a series of studies in the book of Romans for a Bible study group called High Crusaders. This group was connected with Waller High School and met in a home on North Dayton Street in Chicago.

A short time preceding this, evangelist Amy Lee Stockton and her song leader Rita Gould had conducted services at the Belden Avenue Church on North Halsted Street in Chicago. During those meetings, two girls received Christ, and they became the founders of the high school Bible club to which Virginia Latham was invited to speak.

Virginia taught the book of Romans in that amazingly perceptive fashion which was uniquely hers. Cradling her large Bible in her left arm, she spoke of the lost world, barbarian, moralistic, and religious, all lost in sin. She then introduced the Apostle Paul's argument for justification by faith from Romans chapter three, explaining how we were "justified freely by his grace through the redemption that is in Christ Jesus."

The girls who had founded the high school Bible clubs successfully invited their brother to attend those meetings. He listened to the teaching of the book of Romans and, after hearing the message in Romans chapter three, was moved within his soul. That night he stood in a rainstorm and prayed, "Lord, I don't know much about this, but I know that I need Christ. I want now to receive You as my personal Savior, trusting alone in the finished work of Calvary's cross." That night, through the ministry of Virginia Latham, this young man passed from darkness into the light of the gospel.

His name is Dave Breese.

The night was April 11, 1943. I cannot put into words the amazing thing that took place in my life when I understood the gospel of Jesus Christ for the first time. I too, came from a religious background, having been raised by godly parents and throughout all my boyhood years faithfully attending a Methodist Church on Chicago's North Side. I knew the Beatitudes, the Ten Commandments and the books of the Bible. I had a general knowledge of religion and thought of myself as having lived a moral, dedicated life. That night, however, I faced the devastating truth that "all have sinned and come short of the glory of God." My confidence was crushed when I realized that "there is none righteous, no, not one." No person in all the world can claim entrance into heaven or acceptance before a holy God on the basis of his own works. I listened that night with the deepest passion imaginable to the glorious truth that God had provided righteousness in the death of His Son, the Lord Jesus Christ. The words, "being justified freely by his grace through the redemption that is in Christ Jesus" came to my heart like a glorious light from heaven. I saw! I understood!

Through the years that followed their conversion to the Lord Jesus, Lance and Virginia Latham were to bring the message of Christ to thousands of young people and adults. Most of them came from similar religious backgrounds and needed to hear the difference between religion and life in Jesus Christ. The ministry of Lance and Virginia Latham was used of God to call many such young Chicagoans, seeking light and truth, but not finding it until they came to the knowledge of the gospel of Christ. They, too, because of the ministry of this dedicated couple, became heirs of the grace of life.

8

The Tabernacle Days

No one could believe it, but there they were!

Six thousand people had gathered in that new but rustic tabernacle on Chicago's Near North Side during the summer of 1922. The neighborhood around Barry Avenue and North Clark Street looked with astonishment at the crowds that poured off the streetcars and buses, and came on foot from every direction. They rode bicycles, drove, or walked from a distance of miles to the north, west, and south to attend that first meeting in the newly erected tabernacle. "No one will ever know the thrill that came to all of us at hearing that massive crowd sing 'All Hail the Power of Jesus' Name,' " reported a person who was there and who still remembers the new era that had dawned upon Chicago. "It was like heaven, and we knew that God Himself was beginning something that would never stop from this moment on. We knew that God had brought Paul Rader back to Chicago, and the host of people who attended that first night was surely the working of the Lord. It was marvelous in our eyes!"

It had all come about in marvelous fashion. The crusade committee that invited Paul Rader to return to Chicago for a summer evangelistic campaign took a great step of faith. As other cities had done successfully, they, too, chose to erect a large tabernacle to house the meetings. An indication of the faith of the committee is clear from the fact that benches were placed in the tabernacle that would seat six thousand people wall to wall. Sawdust covered the dirt floor and a large platform was put in place that would accommodate a two-hundred-voice choir. Paul Rader had consented to return to Chicago for a campaign that was to last for six weeks. The enthusiastic crowd of saints and sinners who attended that first evening was proof that their faith had not been misplaced.

Another in attendance reports, "The congregational singing was wonderful, the choir was marvelous, the special music was the best that we had ever heard. And then best of all — Paul Rader preached."

The voice of the greatest evangelist of that day rang from the platform pressing the unanswerable question, "What shall it profit a city if it become the biggest in the world and lose its own soul?" He spoke about Chicago; the rumbling, racketeering, exciting and amazing city that Carl Sandburg was later to call "Hog Butcher for the World." Rader's voice rose and fell as he described a city filled with broken hearts, torn families, lost souls, and the other ruins that sin had wrought. The crowd listened in awe, knowing that this man was speaking of the city he loved, indeed the city where he *belonged*.

He quickly lifted outstretched arms of love to the stunned audience and described as only he could the love of Jesus Christ that passes knowledge. He spoke of sin and of judgment to come and then offered the Savior to all who would believe in Him.

"Christ is the answer to the lost souls of Chicago. He stands ready to meet *your* need tonight and to come into *your* heart this evening. Make this the night that you believe the gospel and accept the finished work of Jesus Christ on Calvary's cross as the payment for the penalty of your sin." He pleaded with that audience to respond to

84

the Savior whom he loved and invited them to also receive Jesus Christ as their very own.

As the choir sang, "Come, every soul by sin oppressed, there's mercy with the Lord; and He will surely give you rest by trusting in His word" — they came. From the farthest reaches of that auditorium, they responded to the man standing on the platform and to the Lord Jesus Christ whom he represented. By the hundreds they came to Christ.

This was the beginning. The response was so great night after night that it became apparent to all that a tide of spiritual revival was sweeping again in Chicago. The tabernacle was filled to capacity six nights a week for that six-week crusade.

Everyone agreed that God was doing such a mighty work that the meetings must not stop. They waited upon Paul Rader to continue, for surely the Spirit of God was working in an unprecedented fashion in the heart of Chicago. Paul Rader was obviously a man chosen by God and was the object of the growing and unshakable confidence of great masses of people who were responding to his ministry.

"We are happy to report that Mr. Rader has consented to continue the meetings and stay with us for the next four weeks until Labor Day." A gale of applause swept across the auditorium as people rose to their feet to show their approval with cheers and "Amens!" As the crusade continued, the response was even greater. For the entire ten weeks, capacity crowds came, sang, prayed, and went away moved by the Holy Spirit of God to bring their friends to hear the preaching of the Word. Revival was on.

By the end of that summer, everyone knew that the revival could not be stopped. They recognized that God in singular fashion was visiting the city of Chicago and that a permanent ministry had been formed before their very eyes. Out of that unstoppable crusade, the Chicago Gospel Tabernacle was formed and the era that the world called "The Roaring Twenties" became times of refreshing for Chicago.

Virginia Latham recalls those days. "What a dear man Paul Rader was. I have heard many wonderful preachers and Bible teachers in my lifetime, but none come anywhere near that dear man. The power of God was filling his life and his message drew people to Christ. He was a humble man and never gloried in the crowds that thronged his meetings every night for years. He left the Moody Tabernacle after seven years and Doc traveled with him for a few years. He returned to Chicago at the request of scores of people and built the Tabernacle which stood at Clark Street, Barry Avenue, and Halsted Street. It was to be a temporary structure for one summer but so great were the crowds that they could not stop the meetings."

Many are with us to this day who remember those glorious years of Paul Rader's ministry at the Tabernacle with gratefulness that they can hardly put into words. Thousands still recall with tears of joy what the Lord did.

In those early crowds was a young man by the name of Art Rorheim. Art knew the gospel but came to Christ out of the shock of the death of his brother. Upon receiving the Lord, Art was immediately involved in the tide that touched Chicago in those days. He recalls:

"I look back on the ministry of the Chicago Gospel Tabernacle and I am amazed at what took place in such a short time. I believe the entire Tabernacle ministry was only about fifteen years' duration during Paul Rader's time. My first introduction to it was from my brother, who attended the clubs at the Tabernacle and constantly raved about the tremendous meetings which were taking place. After attending, I understood very well what a tremendous place it was. It was like going to the ball park. People were streaming in from all sides. As we walked into this huge Tabernacle we saw a mammoth platform that held a tremendous band, grand pianos and a great organ that just permeated the air with its beautiful music. Then we would see Paul Rader come, and that great man of God would stand and preach as only he could. As God moved the hearts of thousands of folks, they responded to the message of salvation and dedication with their lives to God's service.

"The Tabernacle was not a beautiful building. It was just a crude structure with large furnaces lined up inside the building, the only means of keeping us warm. The wooden benches and the sawdust floor (which had to be raked occasionally) made the building look anything but ecclesiastical. However, there was something just thrilling about walking into this building. It seemed like the air was spiritually charged."

The personality of Paul Rader was the center of this gigantic impact. Rorheim recalls, "It is evident that the success of the Tabernacle was the ministry of that great man of God, Paul Rader. Even though I was just a boy, I was spellbound when he stepped to the platform and spoke. He had the gift of being able to reach every age group. He could tell stories with a spiritual application like no one I have ever heard. He was an impressive person in stature and stood perhaps six-foot-five. Having been a former boxer and handball player, he used many illustrations from the sports field."

Paul Rader also knew men. He gathered a team of helpers who enabled him to produce programs that made a stunning impact at every meeting of the Tabernacle. There were Clarence and Howard Jones at the trombone and the trumpet. Richard Oliver led the singing, and at the piano and organ were Merrill Dunlop and the young virtuoso who never failed to add sparkle to any song in any key — Lance Latham.

Another friend remembers. "On that immense platform, producing the music from the great organ, music which made the air seem spiritually charged, was Lance Latham. Rader had assembled a platform staff that many feel has never been equaled in any church. The preaching, music and youth ministries were simply incomparable. Many of the young men who were with Rader in those days went on to leadership in the work of Christ that was to be worldwide. One of the men on that platform, leading the choir, playing the trombone, and organizing the youth work that included training hundreds of young people, was the now-famous Clarence Jones. Clarence received his early motivation and inspiration under the ministry of Paul Rader and then moved on to become one of the magnificent missionary statesmen of the world. He is known today as the founder of radio station HCJB in Quito, Ecuador. This was a pioneer work that seemed impossible in the days of its conception."

Lance remembers Clarence Jones, saying, "Clarence and I grew under Paul Rader's ministry. Clarence often said to me, 'Isn't it wonderful how Mr. Rader trusts us to do hard jobs, expects us to carry through, and encourages us?' I was always thankful to count Clarence as one of my best friends for many years and to rejoice in the amazing things that God enabled him to do. I really believe that he had to become the greatest man in radio across the world, secular or otherwise. Think of a man planning a radio station in a South American country where there was no radio, and no radio receivers. He bridged this difficulty by manufacturing his own radio receivers.

"When we visited HCJB a few years ago, we marveled at this wonderful broadcast ministry with its twenty outlets and its staff of almost four hundred

The Pilot Band of the Chicago Gospel Tabernacle, directed by Howard Jones

Richard Oliver and Lance Latham ministered together in the rich musical program of the Chicago Gospel Tabernacle.

Doc and a group of White Shirters, members of the gospel's most interesting brigade.

Howard and Clarence Jones added much to the musical program at the Chicago Gospel Tabernacle.

Naomi Gunderson, Stella Marriott, Myrtle Bergdahl and Virginia Latham started the girls' clubs at the Chicago Gospel Tabernacle, choosing the name and the motto.

workers. We remembered the early days when the vision was in Clarence's heart, and its fulfillment seemed impossible. We rejoice in this work which is always true to the wonderful gospel of grace."

Another man who was part of the Tabernacle youth work in those days was a perceptive lad by the name of Howard Ferrin. Doc recalls, "Howard Ferrin also stands out in my mind as being chiefly influenced through Paul Rader's ministry. We lived together for three years. Both of us can remember with much thanksgiving the many hours spent together in reading and studying our Bibles. Howard Ferrin was on Paul Rader's staff in the early days of the Chicago Gospel Tabernacle and did so much to pave the way for Mr. Rader's ministry there. Howard's dedication and love of the Bible — probably there is no better teacher of Romans — has always been a great inspiration to me."

Howard Ferrin moved to the East to found Providence Bible Institute, now known as Barrington College, a significant Christian educational institution and a magnificent ministry for Christ. The gospel, coupled with the motivation of the unique personality of Paul Rader, continues in Ferrin's ministry to this day.

The ministry of the Tabernacle was sustained in those years by the carefully organized related ministries which developed from the regular Sunday and weekly Tabernacle services. The marvelous musical program under the leadership of Clarence Jones and the preaching of Paul Rader were great central attractions, but soon the Tabernacle had to develop a ministry to those whom Paul thought to be especially important — young people. Rader knew that any future which the work would have must be built on a sustained program of Bible teaching and spiritual challenge to the boys and girls and teenagers who seemed to abound in the endless Chicago neighborhoods. Rader faced the question as to who should be put in charge of this work.

The decision was made — it must be Lance and Virginia Latham. By this time called "Doc" and "Teach," Lance and Virginia assumed the responsibility of developing a club program which would attract young people and contain the ingredients that would bring them to Christ and help them to grow in grace. If the future belonged to young people, they must be reached for Christ now! Lance and Virginia were also convinced that the decision for Christ was only the beginning; young people needed also to be grounded in the Word of God if leadership qualities were going to be produced in their lives.

So they began — there were Flyers, Pioneers and Pilot Clubs for the boys. The girls' clubs were Junior and Senior Guards and Mariners. Meeting times were set and the rudiments of a Bible training program were organized.

Would the new youth programs be attended by the same success as had been seen in the Tabernacle rallies? Trembling at their own inexperience, Lance and Virginia earnestly prayed that God would give them the ability to communicate with young people and the joy of bringing many to salvation and Christian maturity.

Then it happened! Responding to the program in great numbers, boys and girls and teenagers from Chicago's Near North Side gathered about the youthful leadership of the Tabernacle youth program and again the tide began to roll. Hundreds responded, and a new chapter in evangelism was written at the Tabernacle in a unique club program that reached out into the communities, attracting young people from the homes, streets, and alleys of Chicago to come to the Savior. It was apparent that God had given Lance Latham not only an amazing talent for music but a remarkable ability to communicate the saving power of Jesus Christ.

Soon the summer months came, and the question was asked, "What can we do for the boys and girls of Chicago during their vacation time from school?" Once again came a giant step of faith on the part of Paul Rader, responding to the mounting numbers of young people who were gathering about the program at the Tabernacle. He heard of a large conference grounds near Muskegon, Michigan that was for sale. It contained three miles of shoreline on the lake itself and several hundred acres of property, with a few buildings. Paul Rader was convinced that this was the place that God would give them for a summer camping program for the boys and girls of Chicago.

The Sunday came when he preached about the needs of Chicago's young people to the responsive Tabernacle crowd. These people, ordinary wage earners of Chicago, had already given great sums to the program of the Tabernacle and its outreach to Chicago.

"Shall we purchase the conference grounds near Muskegon?" asked Paul Rader. The response once again from the Lord's people was so resounding that the Tabernacle made a commitment of $250,000 for the purchase of the Muskegon property. It was named "Camp Chic-Go-Tab," resembling of course the name of the Chicago Gospel Tabernacle. That summer began the camping ministry of Lance Latham which was to bring him and hundreds of young people to a camping program on every successive summer of his entire life. Tens of thousands of young people who have been brought to the Savior over the years through the camping program can trace the beginnings of that ministry to the faith of Paul Rader and the leadership of Lance Latham beginning in the 1920s.

The Camp Chic-Go-Tab property continues as the Maranatha Bible and Missionary Conference of Muskegon. Howard Skinner became the director in later years of this significant ministry, and the preaching and teaching of the Word of God continued through the depression and World War II.

In recent years, the ministry of Maranatha has experienced a new resurgence under the leadership of Tedd Bryson. The lengthened shadow of Evangelist Paul Rader continues to the blessing of the western Michigan area as a result of that step of faith, well-taken in the purchase of the land for the camping ministry of the Tabernacle.

The Tabernacle also conducted a Bible teaching ministry which enabled thousands of Christians to learn the Word of God in detail and consequently to grow in grace. Wally Warfield remembers, "The Friday night Bible classes at the Tabernacle were marvelous times of blessing from the Lord. People would come by the hundreds, bring their well-worn Bibles, and listen with rapt attention to the careful teaching of Paul Rader or of the youthful Lance Latham. They learned the dispensational truth of C. I. Scofield and understood the gospel of the grace of God like few other congregations in the entire city. The Tabernacle leadership knew that the sustained work of the gospel would only be real as there was a continuing program of Bible study for all. Classes were therefore developed for every age so that everyone might know the Word of God in depth."

Within a few years, Warfield himself was to become a distinguished missionary to Latin America, taking the impetus of those Tabernacle years and carrying it to the lost multitudes of Brazil. Warfield today is the director of the missionary program in the outreach of the Awana Youth Association across the world.

In the midst of the Tabernacle ministry, there broke upon the world a new miracle, and therefore the new challenge of radio. Lance remembers, "Suddenly the announcement was made to the staff that we were to be 'on the air' a week from Sunday from nine in the morning until midnight for a fifteen-hour program. Clarence Jones was to head up the broadcast. A little later the schedule was moderated and it became a twelve-hour program from noon to midnight. The afternoon and evening services would be a part of the all-day program. I had a forty-five minute organ program in the first period and another program later in the day. The 'Sunshine Hour' was half an hour with Roy Johnson as the chief announcer. I had to prepare three other programs. This all-Sunday broadcast, heard over WBBM, continued for nine years."

Mrs. Latham also recalls, "Here our boys' and girls' clubs really started — not called 'Awana' yet. God surely started with nothing when some of us weaklings began clubs for all ages under the guidance of Clarence Jones. We found no shortage of children. When Paul Rader purchased the conference grounds in Michigan, he built two long dormitories and told us to start camps, an activity of which we knew nothing. Somehow when God tells you to do something, you step in, trusting Him, and He adds the ability and strength. What joyous summers we had! We have seen hundreds of kids receive Christ. We did not have much equipment, but we had the Bible, and the gospel which is the power of God unto salvation. Today we stress too much the equipment, surroundings, conveniences, and comforts and are apt to not put enough emphasis on what God alone can and must do through us. We had no hot water or showers, no heated cabins, and outhouses instead of latrines. We went to camp by boat across Lake Michigan, planning our programs on the way over. Camp was real fun; now, with so many conveniences, it gets to be a burden caring for everything; but the Lord has raised up hundreds of wonderful helpers for our camps from many churches."

"We must do our best to reach a dying world," was

also the regular emphasis of Paul Rader. The Tabernacle, in addition to its program of preaching, evangelistic crusades, national radio, youth work, and summer camps, also extended an irresistable call to worldwide Christian groups. Rader envisioned young men riding a new invention of that day — the motorcycle — going everywhere on the face of the earth, preaching the gospel and distributing Christian literature. No young person at the Tabernacle could avoid the earnest call to invest his life to serve Christ across the world.

One of the most marvelous eras that modern Christianity has seen is the nine-year period from 1922 to 1931 in which Paul Rader was used of God to reach Chicago and inspire many others to do the same across the world.

9

A New Challenge in Chicago

That marvelous era lasted for nine glorious years!
From 1922 to 1931, the days at the Tabernacle were
filled with experiences of the blessing and the grace of
God that were to leave their mark on the Christians of
Chicago and ultimately of the world. Many thousands of
people — the young, the old, the poor — a great cross
section of the people of Chicago came to the foot of the
cross under the preaching of Paul Rader and went away
with new life, believing that the blood of Jesus Christ,
God's Son, cleanses from all sin.

From there they went to the ends of the earth. Those
young converts carried the gospel with the help of
established mission boards and sometimes entirely on
their own to Africa, India, China, and the islands of the
sea. Paul Rader backed them up with a ringing call for
new volunteers and for the money to support them. In
one meeting, Rader raised $38,000 for missions, an
enormous sum in those days — in any day. All who came
were reminded that the gospel of the grace of God
implies the responsibility of reaching out across the
world for Christ. Those nine years were a kaleidoscope
of activity, preaching, music, youth work, Bible study,
missions, radio, new ideas, and old methods — all
coming together in a new form of revival which was the
ministry of the Tabernacle.

The gospel was preached, food was served, the needy were cared for, the poor were helped, and sinners were converted by the thousands. So the gospel of Jesus Christ made its permanent stamp upon the life of Chicago and the world.

It also was forever established in the minds and hearts of Lance and Virginia Latham. The vision of the possibility for transforming the lives of people when the gospel of the grace of God was preached was forever printed in their minds. That vision and those possibilities were soon to carry them to the ministry which was to be uniquely their own. Paul Rader had often preached on the subject, "What shall it profit a city if it become the biggest in the world and lose its own soul?" The same message would continue to motivate Doc and Teach.

In 1931, things began to change at the Tabernacle. It was almost as if God had lifted His hand of revival from the ministry there in preparation for similar blessing in a thousand other places under the leadership of those who had seen the great days under Paul Rader.

"Virginia," said Lance, "I believe that God may be leading in a new way in our lives. We should pray that we will know the will of God and the step that He is leading us to take."

So it was that Lance spoke to Virginia about the new conviction that was rising in his heart. The days of the glorious ministry at Chicago Gospel Tabernacle had been magnificent and now it seemed to him as if this era was drawing to a close. The response to the ministry of Paul Rader was still strong, but increasingly Paul was gearing his ministry to the major cities of America. Lance and Virginia had been responsible for the youth work through the years, and multiplied hundreds of young people were looking to them for leadership. From Doc and Teach they heard the unchanged message of the gospel of the grace of God, and from them they received

100

the love that expressed itself in Bible teaching, counseling, and the faithful, sustained ministry. New problems were becoming apparent at the Tabernacle that were both financial and doctrinal. Visiting speakers came from many places to sustain the Tabernacle ministry but somehow it wasn't the same. These developments reinforced mounting conviction in the life of Lance Latham that God was calling them to continue and expand their ministry of the Word of God to Chicago's young people, but in a different place.

Chicago was developing to the west, and the call seemed to come increasingly to Lance and Virginia to establish a work similar to the Chicago Gospel Tabernacle on Chicago's west side.

Their love and loyalty continued unabated to Paul Rader and the Chicago Tabernacle ministry, but they felt they must not be disobedient to the heavenly vision. Out of great concern for a sustained ministry of the gospel of the grace of God in the city of Chicago, they prayed now for the leadership of the Holy Spirit.

Others prayed, and soon the divine direction became apparent. Months later, Lance and Virginia became convinced that they were to start a center of gospel preaching on Chicago's west side.

This was no easy step. Lance recounts those days, saying, "There came a day when we started the North Side Gospel Center. Paul Rader had resigned from the Tabernacle. For a while we did not know where the Lord was leading. There were opportunities in the musical and youth fields but we felt called to the ministry of the Word itself. A group of about fifty young folks met in our home for a prayer meeting and asked if I would be the pastor. Both Mrs. Latham and I felt assured that this was the will of God for us. But how would we start? We had no money."

At this critical point, the Lathams discovered that

where God leads, He also supplies, a principle that they would continue to find true for the rest of their lives. Latham recalls, "The Lord put it on the hearts of friends at Bethel Church, located on Chicago's northwest side, to invite us to use their church on Sunday afternoons. These friends had boys and girls who came to our clubs at the Chicago Gospel Tabernacle and also had attended our camps. They not only invited us, but we were made very welcome. We started with Sunday School at two o'clock in the afternoon, a service at three o'clock, and no meeting in the evening."

The first service was a never-to-be-forgotten experience for the more than three hundred who attended. It was a beautiful Easter afternoon in the year 1933. Everyone who knew Lance and Virginia Latham knew that this new adventure of faith was not a capricious activity. All who attended were sure that this was the beginning of a great new movement of God on Chicago's west side. After hearing the familiar, glorious music to which Chicagoans had become accustomed, they listened attentively to the sermon. Thirty-nine-year-old Lance Latham now moved to the pulpit, addressing his own congregation as the pastor of his own church for the first time in his life. His heart was moved with anticipation of all that God would do as he addressed that congregation from the text, "He that hath wrought us for the selfsame thing is God." "This selfsame thing is resurrection," Lance declared. "We are to live in this world the newness of life which Jesus Christ has purchased for us on the cross by the finished work of Calvary. As we trust Him, we can believe that we as individuals and as this congregation will be enabled to bring the message of a living Christ to this neighborhood and to a lost world." The congregation responded with joy and determined that they would be a part of the working of God in the new ministry called North Side Gospel Center.

Within ten weeks a double-sized store was located on West Fullerton Avenue and the new congregation moved in, renting the store at the depression price of $75 per month. The program was quickly expanded to include afternoon and evening meetings as well as the two o'clock Sunday School.

Lance was the kind of leader who could always inspire loyalty and faithful service on the part of others. Associates gathered to strengthen the hand of Lance Latham in the new Chicago ministry. One of these was the handsome, capable young leader who was to later make his own mark on Chicago, Robert Swanson. Doc remembers him, saying, "Robert Swanson, who had been my valued assistant at the Chicago Gospel Tabernacle, was one of the fifty young folks who invited me to be their pastor. One of the reasons we were able to rent the furniture store on Fullerton Avenue so cheaply was that the building had been damaged by fire. Where Bob Swanson found the forty men and boys who cleaned the building and put it in shape, I do not know. As time went on, he became more and more valuable and not only had charge of the Pioneer Clubs, with over sixty boys turning out, but also held young people's meetings with eighteen-year-olds which soon had an attendance of more than 120."

Bob Swanson worked with Lance in the early years both at the Tabernacle and at the Fullerton Avenue Center. Soon, as could be expected, he was invited to become pastor of a church farther west in the Elmwood Park area. Latham relates, "As much as I hated to lose Bob at the Center, the conviction grew on me that he was worthy of a work of his own. We proposed that he devote his whole time to the Elmwood Park Church and be their pastor."

Others stepped into the ministry at the Center. Soon Art Rorheim, who had been converted under the

Music presented by the choir, orchestra and White Shirt Brigade attracted many neighborhood people to the North Side Gospel Center on Fullerton Avenue.

Congregation sings enthusiastically during an evening service at the Masonic Temple, meeting place of the North Side Gospel Center from 1943-1946.

ministry of Paul Rader, was director of youth activities at the Center. Latham had a remarkable ability to understand men and saw in Art Rorheim the consecration, insight and capacity for diligent labor that would make of him a great leader. He challenged Art to invest his life to reach boys and girls with the gospel of Christ as the greatest single activity in which a person could possibly be involved. "Art, what else can possibly matter in all of this life except winning young people to Christ? You may have many other plans, but I believe God has a special place for you in His service." Art Rorheim responded with joy to that invitation. It was to lead, as we now have seen, to a global youth ministry with the Awana Youth Association that would reach hundreds of thousands of boys and girls like those early groups at the Center.

Art recalls the impact of those conversations with Lance Latham, remembering, "One of the areas that Doc drummed into us was 'Seek ye first the kingdom of God and His righteousness, and all these things shall be added unto you.' He always said, 'Don't let money be a deciding factor as to what God would want you to do. God will always supply, wherever He puts you.' I believe this area of teaching could have been the one factor which changed the course of my life. I was working in a machine shop during the war years. I was married and had two children. Money wasn't easily made during those years. I was in charge of the Pals Club which met on Saturdays at the Center. The company gave us notice that because of the big demand for materials, we would all have to work on Saturdays. This came as a tremendous shock to me. If I were to work on Saturdays, it would mean giving up my Pals Club ministry. The words of Doc kept coming through to my mind and heart, 'Seek ye first the kingdom of God.' I wrestled and prayed with this for several days and finally mustered up enough courage to go and seek out the cruelest boss I had ever known. Since I was a comparatively new employee, I was sure what his answer would be. I walked around his office several times before getting enough courage to make my announcement to him. As I walked into his office, trembling, and sat down, his gruff voice greeted me and said, 'Well, what do you want?' I meekly shared with him that I was directing a youth club, and felt that reaching kids for the Lord was the most important area of my life, and that I wouldn't be able to work on Saturdays, and they would probably have to replace me. To my amazement, he dropped his big cigar, looked in my eyes and said, 'Fellow, I think that what you are doing is just great and I will make an exception for you.' I knew at that time that God had worked a miracle in this man to even cause him to utter those words. I don't believe I would be in Awana today if I hadn't made this decision that Doc had helped me make years before."

Again, the influence of Lance Latham caused the critical turning point in the life of a young man and started him on the path to significant Christian leadership.

From the earliest days at the Center, Doc has chosen boys, one at a time, to work with him at the office. Wally Warfield remembers, "I was the first of those boys who worked and studied with Doc, from the time I was 12 until I was 19. Whenever I was tempted to become involved too deeply in sports at school, he would say, 'Wally, what's first in your life? Service for God or your own fun and pleasure?' I always decided to keep working with Doc. When the call came to leave a good job and go to the mission field, a pattern had been set. Doc's influence in my life made the difference between a life of service for God and a nominal Christian experience."

The beginning days at the Center were difficult in

ways that many would not understand today. Latham recalls those early years, "My salary for two years was $6 a week. I have always been thankful for this experience as I discovered more and more two things. One, the call of God does not depend on how much we get paid, and two, God supplies our needs. I had not been in debt from ten years before that time nor have I been financially embarrassed to the present time."

The way God worked it out for Lance Latham was with an instant expansion of his ministry. He was invited to preach in many like-minded churches across the Chicago area on Sunday mornings. One of his regular ministries was at Grace Missionary Church in Zion, Illinois. The honorarium from the services became a part of his support.

Support also came on a miraculous basis in almost storybook fashion. A friend who was a milkman contributed every week two quarts of milk, a pound of butter and a dozen eggs. A friend in the butcher shop brought leftover meat at the end of the day's activities. The lessons of faith became real in the lives of Lance and Virginia as they trusted God for His support from day to day and rejoiced in His supply.

Recalling further those days, Lance said, "Then to top it off, a good friend, Victor Cory, later head of Scripture Press, recommended to a publishing company that I get out a hymnbook for them. I worked with them on this project and they gave me a royalty of one and one-half cents a copy. The first year that amounted to $600. It was precious to see God's hand in all of this." The hymnbook was "Tabernacle Hymns," still used in churches to this day.

Encouragement came in many forms. Doc recalls, "We owe so much to a member at Bethel Church, Art Hansen, who came shortly after we started and told me, 'The Lord has laid it on my heart to work with you.' A

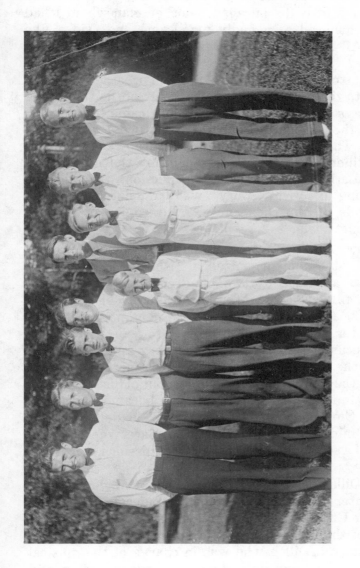

These boys counted it a great privilege to be members of the White Shirt Brigade.

few months later, when the work was not going well and we were a little discouraged, another man whom I had always honored as a godly man came and said a like thing. All of our doubts and fears vanished, *and stayed vanished.*"

So the confidence of Lance Latham breathed a similar faith into the lives of all who were part of the struggling early days at the Center. Victor Cory came to the work and at the same time started Scripture Press Publications. The biblical content of Scripture Press materials was influenced in those early days by the ministry of Lance Latham. His spiritual conviction, through the publishing of Victor Cory, was translated out into thousands of churches and myriad copies of Sunday School materials.

Harry Saulnier came. Harry, always a tireless worker with men, organized a Fishermen's Club that soon was attended by two hundred men every week. These men were constantly encouraged to be witnesses for Christ and helped penetrate the neighborhoods near the Center with their faithful door-to-door witnessing. They became Sunday School teachers and deacons, a part of the dependable fabric of Christian laymen who came to the Center. Harry Saulnier, out of his continuing concern to reach men and their need, became director of Pacific Garden Mission. Under his leadership, this notable ministry has grown to the place where it is a model of a soul-winning lighthouse to missions across the nation.

Bill Dillon came to the Center. Under his leadership, the Center established a radio broadcast on Station WIND in Chicago every Saturday night. Latham recalls, "I do not think we realized at the time what a treasure we had in Bill Dillon who was in charge of the musical program. The program included an ensemble of mixed voices, a brass quartet, and our White Shirt Brigade, with Ed Sherry, a young man about twenty years of age, as our announcer. The program expanded and moved to Station WAIT and continued for more than eight years."

Bill Dillon became the director of Sunshine Gospel Mission with a great ministry to the derelicts of Chicago. Sunshine Gospel Mission did at the north end of the Loop a similar work to that which was done at Pacific Garden Mission at the south end of the Loop. Bill Dillon's son Bill, Jr. has now established an urban ministry called Inner City Impact on Chicago's near west side. Many have been converted to Christ in this "impossible area" of Chicago under his leadership.

Ed and Sally Sherry became a part of the program. These two became the "piano team" of the Center, helping to make it one of the great musical programs in the city of Chicago. Ed and Sally continue to this day in their faithful, creative musical ministry at the Center.

No single book can adequately describe the new fountainhead of ministry which began to pour blessings upon the city of Chicago at the Center. Those who were a part of the work in those days will always remember the song leading and solo work of Henry Holmbo, joyous, round-faced song evangel. They thrilled to the unique music of the White Shirt Brigade. They knew that God had sent Rudy Levey to lead the Center orchestra. Ray Bayne, then a student at McCormick Theological Seminary, came to conduct the music program.

All would agree that the major force in the ministry of the Center was the faithful preaching of the gospel of the grace of God by Lance Latham. There was something insistent and forceful about his ministry that made every hearer know that he was not listening to sermons by an ordinary minister.

Significant to them was William R. Newell. The congregation had often sung his best known hymn, "At Calvary." They anticipated that Newell was coming and listened with attention to his incomparable expositions of the gospel of the grace of God. His ministry created further maturity in biblical understanding on the part of Lance Latham. Newell's book, *Romans, Verse by Verse,* became almost required reading to those who heard his preaching.

William Pettingill came to the ministry of the Center. Again his faithful expositions of the gospel of the grace of God extended beyond the biblical comprehension of the Center congregation. They knew the message of the gospel was not some local invention but that it represented a true understanding of God's Word.

The preaching of the Word created a dynamism, a life at the Center that could not help but explode its influence in a thousand directions. Lance Latham would be the first to testify that it was not any man, it was the message of the gospel of the grace of God that did it. The testament of grace that was the life of Lance Latham now had taken shape and form for all to see. Within a few short years, the ministry of the North Side Gospel Center was on solid footing. It seemed, as it ministered in Chicago, to be the fulfillment of the promise, "Where sin abounded, grace did much more abound."

10

A Doorway to Heaven

"What is this place — this North Side Gospel Center? Is it a church, a cult, a mission? Who do these people think they are? What goes on here?"

So it was that one pastor of a staid Chicago church expressed the questions that many had as they heard about or saw the activities centered around the new and growing congregation on Chicago's west side. The years that followed the 1933 opening of the North Side Gospel Center brought a high percentage of the Christians of Chicago at one time or another to visit the remarkable meetings on Sunday afternoon at the Center. Many would come following their attendance at a liberal or cold denominational church in the morning and could not help but mark the contrast between the deadness of their religious involvements and the obvious, the thrilling life that characterized the meetings at the Center. Happy people were there, rejoicing in the Lord. The song service was a glorious experience and the special music was even more uplifting. When the choir rose to sing, their musical impact was almost a physical experience. Then moving onto the platform would be a group of boys wearing white shirts and bow ties whom Lance introduced as the White Shirt Brigade. They sang as if their lives depended upon it.

Then the band would play. Under the leadership of Bill Dillon or Rudy Levey, the band would strike up a martial tune that usually came from the old band book, "Billy Sunday's Favorite Songs." Everyone enjoyed the Center orchestra except occasionally Ray Clasen, now a medical doctor, who would say, "Not good, but loud."

But especially there was the preaching, and that was unquestionably the real secret of the success at the Center. By any standard, the musician and youth leader, Lance Latham, was turning into a most unusual and effective preacher of the gospel. Probably no one would ever call him eloquent, but no one could resist the overwhelming impression that he *meant* every word that he said. They also were persuaded that he had the deepest possible concern for the eternal destiny of every young person and adult who came to hear him.

And they came by the hundreds. They came most of all to hear his message, the imperative truth that again and again he called "the gospel of the grace of God." No one of us who was in those meetings will forget the intensity with which Doc denounced all other alternatives except salvation by faith in the finished work of Christ alone.

"Your religion will not save you," he insisted. "Some of you are still trapped in the damnable tentacles of your wretched denomination which has long since denied the faith and turned to that hideous soul-destroying religion of liberalism. If you continue on this course, you will die and go to hell! It's time to get out of that religious prison that entraps you every Sunday morning and discover the freedom of salvation that is available to you because Jesus died for you."

He would then continue on another line, enforcing his points with his thin, knuckled hand rapping on the pulpit. "Some of you poor souls are trying to make it to heaven on the basis of your own works. Haven't you ever read the Apostle Paul who said, 'Now to him that worketh is the reward not reckoned of grace, but of

114

debt'? Don't you realize that if we could be saved by works, then Jesus would never have had to die for us? Your works can only damn you and send you to hell. You must come and be saved by grace or you cannot be saved at all!"

On those Sunday afternoons and Sunday evenings, Latham preached the whole counsel of God, but usually returned to the message of justification by the grace of God based on the third chapter of Romans. Paul Rader had become the second Paul in his life, but the first Paul would always be Paul the Apostle. The gospel of the grace of God and not the gospel of works would be his recurring theme in every message.

How wonderfully God used that message! Young people and adults who came to listen felt their religious confidence slip away from them like sinking sand. The hammer of the Word of God destroyed their artificial foundations and they saw themselves as desperate sinners without hope. Week after week, month after month they reached out from the hopelessness of their false, sophisticated Protestant religion to the glorious liberty of Jesus Christ. Christians are all across the world today who never will forget how they came to the Savior through the message of the gospel of the grace of God preached by Lance Latham in those early days at the Center.

One friend said, "It was only a furniture store, but it became the doorway to heaven to people who gathered by the hundreds in those days. To those of us who first became aware of the ministry of Lance Latham in the West Fullerton Avenue location, the North Side Gospel Center had a different 'feeling' to it. It wasn't quite like a church, and yet the sense of the presence of God was more real than in most of the churches which we knew."

Hundreds came, some invited by friends, some out of curiosity, some in pursuit of the rumors that "something was going on here" of which they ought to be a part.

The Center quickly became known as a church with an endless variety of programs. No tiny tot, teenager, young adult, or older person was without a program paying special attention to his particular needs. One visitor said, "I was astonished at the quality of people who attended the Center. Everyone seemed so talented, so articulate, so *alive* that I felt this church was a cut above most of the old, staid religious gatherings which I had known."

Above many things the story of the Center was the story of youth. The church had been organized by a basic nucleus of fifty young people, most of whom had a background at the Chicago Gospel Tabernacle. They were in their teens and early twenties and almost all had been converted under the ministry of Paul Rader or Lance and Virginia Latham. They were convinced that the gospel of Christ would have the same appeal to other young people who would have the opportunity to hear. The first teenager to come to the meetings from the Center neighborhood was Hank Reuter, later to become Art Rorheim's brother-in-law. The young people responded with instant enthusiasm to the programs centered around the first necessity of winning young people to Christ and teaching them the Word of God so they could develop into Christian leaders.

Lance and Virginia looked back at their experience at the Chicago Gospel Tabernacle and translated the lessons learned as "weaklings" in those days into the Center.

Doc remembers, "We felt we must have a program that would appeal to young people, reaching them for Christ and teaching them the Word so they could develop Christian maturity. Having learned from Paul Rader the lesson that in order to succeed, you must grow your own leadership, we immediately organized youth clubs for boys in three age groups, Pals, Pioneers and Pilots."

Working by her husband's side, Virginia met with the girls who would become leaders in the girls' work at the Center. Three groups corresponding to the ages of the boys were decided upon. They were Chums, Junior Guards, and Senior Guards. "We still felt that we knew little about how to work with young people," says Virginia, "but we were sure that we would have the help of God in performing the ministry to which the Lord had called us."

So it was that the upstairs rooms at the Center, which included meeting-places in the small gymnasium, were filled night after night with bright-eyed boys and girls who attended the weeknight youth club programs. Few buildings in the history of the world that were ever used for religious purposes were used more fully and more exhaustively than was the furniture store that became the North Side Gospel Center. Young people were there simply *all* of the time. They came straight from school in the afternoon to help in painting, putting up signs, running a mimeograph, or calling others on the phone. They would pick up fliers for advertising the meetings the following Sunday or a coming evangelistic campaign and take them out to distribute to the neighborhood. Unpaid volunteer workers labored into the late hours many evenings, preparing the needed materials for the next meeting.

Bill McGarrahan was an illustration of this. When he came to the Center to conduct a youth crusade, the needed props were unbelievable. One evening a full-sized whale was constructed all across the platform as McGarrahan told the story of Jonah to a packed auditorium of astonished boys and girls. On another night, a river was "constructed" as McGarrahan told the story of the healing of Naaman the leper. Bill spoke at

Members of the first Pals Club stand proudly in front of the North Side Gospel Center on Fullerton Avenue.

Pal Club leaders wear the early club insignia, a red neckerchief.

the first Fairmont Fair in 1938 at the Center, and Art Rorheim considers him the finest children's evangelist he knows. Because the Pal Club members enthusiastically invited friends from school, 325 boys crowded into the limited facilities at the Center on that occasion.

No one could be a part of that program without sensing that, as exciting as were the externals, the foundation of it all was the Word of God and the preaching of the gospel. No meeting of any kind was complete without an earnest presentation of the Scripture and an invitation to receive Christ as personal Savior. Around this program gathered great numbers of young people, but also in the midst of it emerged some of the most faithful leaders who have ever served in the work of the gospel. "We never could have done it," reports Virginia Latham, "without the help of those dear young people who committed themselves to serve so faithfully with us. Many were still in their high school years, but because of the Word of God, they developed that early maturity and leadership capability which made them dependable teachers and workers for the Lord."

Those leaders knew that they were "a collection of nobodies," as one of them said, but they served like veterans. By contrast to the difficulties of other churches in getting people to lead, the Center developed leaders in great numbers. With Lance and Virginia, those early leaders met to prayerfully consider the principles that would produce success in the youth work in the Center. They were sure that God would bless if they followed these principles.

1. The program must be centered around the gospel. There are many other youth organizations which young people can attend. Their work is of lesser value unless it introduces young people to Christ and leads them to believe in the finished work of

the cross. The message is grace! We are saved by grace through faith plus nothing.

2. It must have a high scriptural content. The Bible can be the most interesting study in the world if properly presented. A knowledge of the Word of God is the only thing that really produces growth in grace, maturity. Let us teach and inspire young people to memorize the Bible. Without Bible memorization, you do not know the Scripture!

3. It must be attractive to young people. The dreary programs that were sponsored by many churches would never succeed at the Center. There must be games, promotion, prizes. Make it fun for the kids. Lord, save us from the terrible sin of sameness. Young people will drop out unless they sense variety and the planning that keeps a program current and interesting.

4. It must be built on the leadership. Without bright people running the meeting and organizing the programs, things will begin to wander. Mere discussion groups are mostly a waste of time. Experiment with new leadership at the edge of your program, but put your most dependable people in charge of the important sessions. The quality of your leadership will make or break you.

5. It must develop leadership as quickly as a young person shows spiritual potential. Give him an opportunity to do something, have him preach a sermon, lead a song, give him a Sunday School class to teach. The program that does not develop leadership cannot be considered a success. Our purpose is to bring everyone from the point of faith in Christ into Christian maturity.

"Put the thrill into it," said Lance Latham. "Dry, starchy programs and endless catechisms may well represent the truth, but no one will respond. Remember, everything that you do must be done heartily as unto the Lord." With these and many other admonitions, the tireless Lance Latham became the driving force of one of the most effective youth programs on a church level that Chicago had ever seen. The results became immediately apparent as hundreds attended and many stepped out of darkness into the marvelous light of the gospel.

Ed Dubisz came into the Center and was invited to a boys' club. Raised in a religious background, he knew nothing of the gospel. Within a few weeks, Ed received Christ and now serves his Lord as a missionary in Central Africa.

Rich Wager came. He heard the marvelous story of the gospel and knew that he must then and there become a Christian. He accepted Christ and soon stepped into early leadership opportunities which the Center afforded. Rev. Richard Wager is now the pastor of Emmanuel Baptist Church of Berwyn, Illinois and director of Silver Birch Ranch in Wisconsin.

Harold and Jimmy Barker came. They were invited to the meeting by one of the Pal leaders and there they heard the story of the cross and received Christ. James Barker is now a missionary in South America and Harold is pastor of the First Baptist Church in Watseka, Illinois.

John Stahl came. Attracted by the athletic program and the vibrant young people he met, he stayed to listen to the gospel. John Stahl received Christ. He served on the mission field in Brazil and now is a full-time executive with the Awana Youth Association.

The whole Mielke family came. There the Lord stirred their hearts. Elaine is now Mrs. Cameron Townsend, wife of the founder of Wycliffe Bible Translators. Dan is a Christian businessman whose son is a missionary in New Guinea.

Bob Williams came to the Center. Here he heard the marvelous message of the grace of God and received Christ. Bob now serves as a missionary in Borneo in the South Pacific.

Russ Killman came. He now directs the "Heaven and Home Hour" broadcast from California.

Dave Breese came to the Center. He saw the contrast between this and his denominational background. Having accepted Christ under the ministry of Virginia Latham, he moved into the Center program. He now serves Christ as an evangelist. The ministry of the North Side Gospel Center in that Fullerton Avenue location made the most dramatic impact upon his personal life imaginable.

Jack Frizen came. Inspired by the Center program, he committed his life to serve Christ. He is now national chairman of the Independent Fundamental Missionary Society, organizing and directing missionary activity to many lands across the world.

The young people came from everywhere. There seemed to be no end to the supply of enthusiastic teenagers who poured in from the corners of Chicago. The story is the same with the girls. Attracted by the power of the gospel and moved by the ministry of Mrs. Lance Latham, they came from everywhere and were saved. They invested their lives for Christ and their story is legion.

Soon Art Rorheim was called upon to take a giant step of faith. He left his job and came on the Center staff as its full-time youth director. In the providence of God, Art had been given amazing ability to understand young people, to fashion programs that would motivate them and to conserve the results of evangelism in the training of Christian leaders.

Lance and Virginia met regularly with the youth leaders in every department. Unforeseen problems were discussed, prayed over, and new decisions were made. There was no precedent for such youth activities. Programs were invented out of thin air, games perfected, approaches sharpened by leaders who were involved to the hilt in the actual doing of youth work.

"Let me give you a principle which has worked down through the years," said Lance to his leaders. "It is this. Always work with your best young people. Fashion your program to stimulate the sharpest, brightest, and the most spiritual. Don't ever let your youth program sink to the lowest denominator where you are trying to please everybody. Make demands upon the young people and they will rise to them. Keep them all in mind, of course, don't neglect anyone; but let the central thrust of your program be to the finest of the kids." Paul Rader had instilled that principle into his mind and thinking many years before so that now it reproduced itself in the quality of the youth program at the Center. All who looked on the ministry of the North Side Gospel Center knew that the central thrust was the gospel of the grace of God. They also knew that the major strategy was to reach and win young people. No one doubted that here was the church with a future.

11

The Gospel's Most Interesting Brigade

"Stick 'em up!"

As Doc drove his loaded automobile to Michigan City, the boys in the back seat cooked up a little scheme. Ches Hanson crawled out of the back window, unnoticed by Doc in his concentration on the highway ahead. As the speeding car moved down the highway, muscular young Hanson pulled himself around the back of the car. He clung to the spare tire and drew himself over the fender onto the left running board. Then he moved up next to the driving Mr. Latham, put his finger against his head and shouted, "Stick 'em up!" The eight boys in the car roared with laughter at Doc's consternation. Latham wondered, not only at the event, but how Hanson was able to accomplish it as the car careened down the highway. Sometimes the boys would even cover Doc's eyes while he was driving and ask, "Guess who?"

Everyone agreed that these lads could have been into more shenanigans than even the long-suffering Lance Latham could keep up with. Yet before the day was done, they would stand like cherubs and sing their way into the hearts of the delighted audience.

This was the White Shirt Brigade.

The calls came from everywhere, "Doc, come over to Michigan and help us!" "Doc, can we get you and the boys to come up here and give us a meeting in Milwaukee? Everybody has heard about you and we know we could get a great crowd." The story of the amazing development that the North Side Gospel Center in Chicago had in its remarkable traveling group of boy singers, the White Shirt Brigade, had reached out to the entire Middle West.

Christianity has had many traveling musical groups, but few more interesting or charming than this group of fifteen to eighteen boys. When appearing at a church, the White Shirt Brigade was a rare phenomenon indeed. Here was a group of boys from eight to eighteen years of age opening up in a refreshing, hearty chorus of four-part harmony. The White Shirt Brigade became one of the favorite musical groups of most of the Midwest cities.

Doc had organized this group of boys for the purpose of adding that needed musical attraction to meetings everywhere. Through the first ten years of the life of the North Side Gospel Center, Christianity's most interesting brigade, Lance Latham's White Shirts, traveled thousands of miles and became the darlings of admiring crowds everywhere. Arne and Donny Tweten were called "Tweedledee and Tweedledum." "They can sing like nobody's business," someone said, "and they always bring down the house." Crowds everywhere were astonished at the ability of the boys to recite in chorus the first eleven verses of Hebrews 12. Then they would sing their famous number,

I saw a blood-washed pilgrim,
A sinner saved by grace,
Upon the King's great highway,
With peaceful, shining face.
He said, 'The yoke is easy,
The burden, it is light.'

Temptations sore beset him
But nothing could affright.

Any meeting that promised the piano and organ artistry of Lance Latham, the music of the White Shirt Brigade, a trumpet solo by Howard Jones, and then a message by Doc was almost always guaranteed a full house.

John Stahl, one of the members of the White Shirt Brigade now on the executive staff at Awana Headquarters, remembers those years. "An interesting area of Doc's life was his unique success in working with young people. Strange as it may seem, his talents were not in the area of sports and outdoor activities, but he was very successful for over fifty years in Christian camping. His real talent was music. He organized young people into singing groups. There were kids from many different backgrounds in the neighborhoods of Chicago.

"The White Shirt Brigade took its name from the starched, white, long-sleeved shirts worn with a black bow tie, fitted around well-scrubbed faces and necks. Doc recruited the White Shirters from his newly organized church and boys' clubs and came up with a steady attendance of forty or more boys in each Saturday morning practice." Imagine, forty boys meeting on a Saturday morning in order to develop their talents to sing for Christ!

"The White Shirt Brigade was organized for several purposes by Doc," mentions Stahl. "They would aid the new ministry on Radio Station WIND and the "Lifeline" program. He utilized the talents of the White Shirts whenever possible to provide much of the music needed before the gospel message. For his vision in Christian camping, the White Shirt Brigade concerts helped to promote financial support for the camps. Doc had a teaching ministry to the boys themselves in the White

Arne and Don Tweten, known as "Tweedledee and Tweedledum", sang many duets while traveling with the White Shirt Brigade.

Many Midwest churches enjoyed the four-part harmony of the White Shirt Brigade.

**Ed and Sally Sherry, Merrill Dunlop, and Lance Latham
were the regular participants in the four piano concerts.**

Shirt Brigade. He realized that he had a captive audience listening to the great truths from the Bible as the boys sat through the speaking portion of their singing engagements. The continual repetition of the gospel of grace may have fallen on some deaf ears in the audiences. This repetition, however, would continue to work in the hearts and lives of many of the boys and reap eternal dividends."

In his ministry with the White Shirt Brigade, we see another lesson which can be learned from the life of Lance Latham. He never did anything just for amusement or window dressing. Every activity had to have a spiritual purpose and an opportunity to teach the gospel. This ministry bore marvelous fruit in the lives of the young men who were then a part of the White Shirt Brigade.

Another White Shirt Brigader remembers, "Coming from the post-depression era, it was a unique experience for these boys to be selected by Doc to go with him on White Shirt dates. It meant travel, staying in strangers' homes, and visiting areas normally out of the reach of city-bound kids. They learned what limits Doc set on their behavior, but had their own ways of keeping things interesting for themselves and others."

The boys remember that startling things happened at the homes where the White Shirt Brigade stayed overnight. Once a lovely Christian hostess was surprised to see a picture on the wall of her living room come crashing to the floor. She wondered about the commotion upstairs and didn't realize that Doc was conducting a wrestling match with a couple of the kids.

But what a ministry they conducted! One White Shirter remembers, "Even stiff churches applauded the Tweten brothers as they sang their duets. Soloists like Billy Talbot and Hank Christensen sang 'The Holy City.' Hank Holmbo was also a favorite soloist and song leader, emceeing many of the performances."

The music of the White Shirt Brigade programs included more than the singing of the boys themselves. Lance Latham, we must remember, was one of the most accomplished organists in the Christian world. He was often called upon to play an organ which had never been used to its fullest extent. The people would listen, spellbound, to his rendition of "The Storm" and other great Christian numbers. Many small churches had never heard such music. The program included everything from "Jesus, Savior, Pilot Me" to the stirring Sousa march "Stars and Stripes Forever." There were frequent standing ovations for the music of Lance Latham and the White Shirt Brigade.

It was not unusual for the White Shirt Brigade to have 150 separate dates in the course of a year. This meant sacrifice on the part of the boys. It was nevertheless counted one of the great privileges of life to be a part of this group.

The story of the ministry of Lance Latham continued for all of his life to be the story of music. In the providence of God, the training in his childhood home was now being translated into the hearts and lives of multitudes of people.

The remarkable musical program at North Side Gospel Center developed other musical ideas which were unknown at that time. No one will ever forget the four-piano concerts. For more than forty successive years a capacity crowd gathered at the Center, and still does, to hear the two-night special presentations of the four pianos. The regular four participants have been Lance Latham, Ed and Sally Sherry, and Merrill Dunlop. Occasionally the variant piano quartet would include Dennis Moffat, June Hedman, Barbara Mitchell, Ernie Meyer, Lillian Jones, Mildred Dillon, or Helen Lyle.

Many musicians and groups had their start at the

Center, learning there the lessons which made a great ministry possible. Lance has always been very sure that a great part of the ministry of God in the lives of Christians took the form of "psalms and hymns and spiritual songs, singing and making melody in your heart to the Lord."

Doc composed music for several hymn poems by Avis B. Christiansen, including "Only Jesus" and "Blessed Calvary!" Campers down through the years have joyously sung "When You Get the Love of Jesus in Your Heart", a melody composed by Doc to fit words by Howard Jones. Church choirs still sing from *Tabernacle Choir Number Two,* compiled by Lance Latham. Music for the four-piano concerts has always been arranged by Doc and rehearsed under his direction.

The music that Lance Latham learned under the tutelage of his mother before he was five years old was to be used for greater purposes than even she could have suspected. Few ministries have had the quality and variety of music that has always been presented at the Center. "The music program alone is enough to make anybody want to come to these amazing meetings," said one admirer of the work. "But everybody knows that the music, great as it is, is only a part of the larger picture and the greater purpose. That greater purpose is the life-changing message, the gospel of the grace of God."

In a pensive moment when Lance and I were speaking, he once said to me, "Dave, only the Lord saved me from music." I had just been listening to 15 minutes of Beethoven played by Lance himself on the piano at his home before dinnertime. I will never forget how Doc then turned to me and said those words, "Only the Lord saved me from music." The truth of the matter is that the Lord Jesus saved both Lance Latham and his music, committing both to a greater purpose than they ever could have known at the beginning.

12

Camp For Me

She looked beautiful with the firelight flickering across her face!

This seventeen-year-old girl — a Senior Guard — was thinking deeper thoughts than she had ever known before. Yes, she was from a church background, but what about this necessary thing of receiving Christ, of whom she had heard this evening? As she stared into the fire, there came across her heart a pensive longing for spiritual reality.

"Susie, dear, let's talk together; perhaps I can help." The speaker was the willowy, winsome lady who had just been speaking to 200 girls around that camp fire about the Lord Jesus Christ. Mrs. Lance Latham — "Teach" herself — sat down next to the girl. Teach opened her well-worn Bible and then proceeded to explain how Jesus Christ died for our sins and how by faith in Him we have everlasting life. Susie could see love written upon the face of the lady who spoke and could feel her own heart responding with understanding to the gospel. She bowed her head and through quiet tears prayed, "Lord, I know that I am the sinner for whom Jesus died and I want to receive Him now as my Savior." There was rejoicing in heaven once again as another soul stepped out of darkness into the marvelous light of the gospel. Susie's T-shirt read "Camp Awana," and she would never, not for all of eternity, forget what had happened to her there that night.

This teenager was typical of the now tens of thousands of boys, girls, young people, and adults who have been a part of the camping programs which have come out of the ministry of Lance Latham. From the very first, camping has been a part of that ministry.

"It is foolish to believe that a half-hour session at Sunday School will do the job in the life of a young person," Lance Latham has said. "The problems of the world are too great and the knowledge of the Word of God is too necessary a thing just to leave it all up to a Sunday School program."

Lance and Virginia Latham were always of the conviction that the gospel of the grace of God was serious business. Being a Christian and living for Christ was not merely a part of life...it was life itself. It seemed to them therefore somewhat absurd that something so important as being a Christian was a small involvement for people on a Sunday morning. They would never concur that it would be possible for a person to learn the Word of God in sufficient manner to be a strong Christian merely by Sunday School exposure.

They were convinced that young people would achieve maturity and leadership only if they were under a concentrated program of Bible study and related Christian activities. The solution...summer camp. So it was that from the earliest days, the Lathams were involved in bringing in people from the streets and alleys of Chicago to an unforgettable, two-week camping experience. Thousands of Midwest young people now serving Christ as mature Christian adults will testify that their conversion to Christ or consecration to the Savior came as a result of being at a camp with Lance or Virginia Latham.

The first camp was "Chic-Go-Tab" on Lake Michigan,

near the city of Muskegon, Michigan. Paul Rader purchased this as a camp and conference grounds in the early 1920s. When the North Side Gospel Center was organized in the early 1930s, it was inevitable that camps would constitute the summer program. Until 1939, the location near Muskegon, Michigan continued to be the campsite although the name was changed to "Michidune." Then a campground owned by the state of Michigan near Kalamazoo, in a place called Yankee Springs, was rented for the summer and operations began under the name of "Camp Michawana."

The name Michawana was not chosen just because it has a flowing Indian sound. "Awana" was a careful choice, and the letters stand for "*A*pproved *W*orkmen *A*re *N*ot *A*shamed." This centered on the theme verse which was the Apostle Paul's admonition to the young Timothy, "Study to show thyself approved unto God, a workman that needeth not to be ashamed, rightly dividing the word of truth" (II Timothy 2:15).

The camp programs, as thousands of former campers will recall, consisted of great athletics, delicious food, unforgettable fun, but above all, interesting and challenging Bible study. The average camper memorized twenty to thirty verses during the two-week session at camp and was involved in a course of study in a book of the Bible — Romans, Revelation, Hebrews — something that was easily comparable to a Bible course on a college level. Lance Latham was convinced that young people needed to know the Word, or else they would be vulnerable to the attacks of Satan. He considered it irresponsible to pretend to be a youth worker and not have a program with its first emphasis on Bible study and Scripture memorization. So the program at Camp Michawana became the foundation of Bible understanding and spiritual development for thousands of people.

This dormitory was the first building constructed at Chic-Go-Tab, later called Camp Michidune.

Doc and Teach took a group from Camp Awana on a special outing to the Wisconsin Dells.

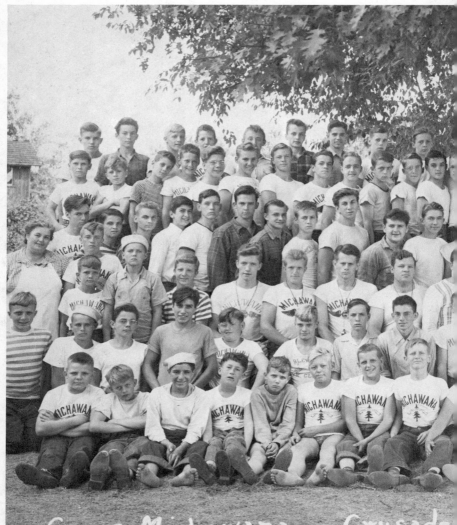

Camp Michawana — Crusade

44

Wise-Hastings

cluded in this remarkable picture taken at Camp Michawana in 1944
e at least 25 boys who today serve the Lord in full-time Christian
nistries.

By the middle 1940s, it became apparent that other and larger plans would need to be made for the summer camp program for the boys' and girls' clubs at the North Side Gospel Center and other churches.

No description could be more graphic than Lance Latham's own remembrance of the crossroads and the crisis that now developed in the camping program. These were days when money was short but faith was large, and the scenario from this point reads like an adventure story.

"We held camp for the boys and girls from the opening days of our church in a rented camp. The time had come for us to have a camp of our own. The wonderful camp that we had in Michigan was rented from the state of Michigan which was restricting our use of it more and more to Michigan campers.

"While we were looking to the Lord to find us a place, I received a call from George Ziemer, the pastor of the Wisconsin Tabernacle which Paul Rader had founded some years before. He was a man whole-heartedly with us in caring for young folks." The message was, "I had answered an ad in the Milwaukee paper about a property of 123 acres located on a small inland lake in Wisconsin. The real estate man called me and said, 'I have received 120 answers to my ad today. Yours is the 120th I have read, and the only one that said anything. I want to offer you the first chance at this property.'" Mr. Ziemer's letter which had prompted this offer was, "We want a place to teach boys and girls the Bible and to lead them to Christ."

"An answer which might have caused opposition was one great link in our Camp Awana today. Mr. Ziemer said that I must come up and see the property. So two or three of our men, Mrs. Latham and I, went the same day and saw the beautiful site which has proved so ideal for a camp, now for over thirty years.

"The only difficulty was that we had no money. I was still paying on a house and seldom had over $100 in the bank. The wife of the owner said she would wait until the following Monday for an answer. The price was only $15,000. I was over at our Michigan camp when Mr. Ziemer called on Saturday and said, 'You'd better decide now or you may lose it.' I felt we had no other course than to say yes. On returning to the Center on Monday, I told the board what I had done — that I felt I had no other choice. I had an idea of four places from which $15,000 might come. The only one that materialized was the Center, with $2,500. With a $500 down payment, the owner of the property gave us six weeks to come up with the amount necessary. We had $5,000 by that time, and naturally went with some fear that this would not be acceptable. To our surprise she said, 'My husband drinks and gambles and I would much rather take part of the amount this time, for I am afraid he will gamble it all away.' So we were glad to comply with her request.

"Due to the request of a friend of mine, a bank in West Bend loaned us $20,000 at four percent interest. Two men who turned out to be wonderful friends were directors of the bank. Mr. Altendorf, the president and Mr. C. J. Schloemer, who was at that time mayor of West Bend, told me afterwards, 'We at our bank appreciated hearing what you were going to do and wanted to make you a gift from the bank. Our rules made this impossible, so we made you a loan at the lowest interest rate that we are allowed.' We were thus enabled to pay the amount due for the property.

"I do not know that I was prepared for what it would cost us at camp the following year. That cost was not $15,000, but $57,000.

"At that time I was teaching Bible classes for New Tribes Mission, which at that time had headquarters in Chicago. I was teaching three hours, three times a week;

then, in addition, had a three-hour conference with Paul Fleming and the other workers every Friday afternoon. I naturally felt that with the opening of the new camp three to four months away, I had to cut out one of the three days.

"The Lord very definitely impressed upon me, 'You attend to my business; I'll attend to yours.' Never in my life have I seen as much take place in four months.

"In March, before camp was to open, there were five old buildings on the grounds, besides the farmhouse and barn. This could possibly take care of about thirty people; camp would probably open with over 170. It was at the end of the second World War, and one could not even make an application for a permit to build. It seemed impossible to even buy lumber.

"I searched around for lumber. One day at the New Tribes headquarters a man was telling Paul Fleming that he wanted some folks to tear down a four-story house. I ventured to say to him, 'Will you let us tear it down and sell the lumber to us?' He answered, 'No, but I know where you can get some lumber.' He told of a shipment coming from a firm in Elgin. He said that if we left right away, we could probably get some. One of our men found that the company would sell us three truckloads of lumber for $2,500. Our men encouraged me to accept the offer. The only difficulty was that I didn't have the $2,500.

"Merrill Dunlop and I were giving a special night of music at George Ziemer's tabernacle in Milwaukee. I told him of our situation. George said that there was a woman in his church who wanted to give him $2,500 with the condition that he pay her $100 a month so she would have a fixed income for two years. I thought, 'That's fine, but it doesn't help me.' After the evening music was over, George said, 'Lance, if you want me to, I'll ask her if you can *have* that $2,500 as a gift.' We phoned the lady and she gave us the money that night.

"Early the next morning we purchased the lumber. As the third truck was leaving, the foreman shouted, 'You can't take that lumber away!' Now the owner 'happened' to be there at that early hour and said, 'Oh, let them have it; what's the difference?' "

Here Doc reminds himself and all of us of the providence of God that presided over all of these details. Those of us who were a part of the camping program in those days will never get over the sense of adventure in all of it. I was in the room when George Ziemer's original call came through and joined the prayer meeting that followed in which we trusted the Lord for His leadership.

Doc continues to recall the miraculous developments that transpired. "And all of this at a time when no applications for permits were available! When I was in Milwaukee a few days later, George Ziemer called my attention to an article in the paper which said that applications to build were being granted if certain conditions were met. I went to the application office, told them what our plans were and showed them some pictures. He asked me, 'Have you got your footings in?', for this was a necessary condition. I told him that no footings were in but we had three truckloads of lumber on the grounds. I said to him, 'Does that look as if we mean business?' He said, 'Yes,' and then came the first word of hope. 'Would you be willing to use cement instead of wood for your cabin floors?' I said 'Anything, just so we can go ahead.' That afternoon we received a permit with no restrictions.

"In the arrangement for a loan from the bank, we were obligated on a certain day each year to pay back $2,000 with interest. On one occasion when this was due, I visited a friend and asked him to pray with us about our financial need. He smiled encouragingly and said, 'Lance, I'd be happy to loan you $2,000 for a while.'

Doc's unique ministry among hundreds of campers down through the years was recognized by Christian Camping International as this plaque was presented to him.

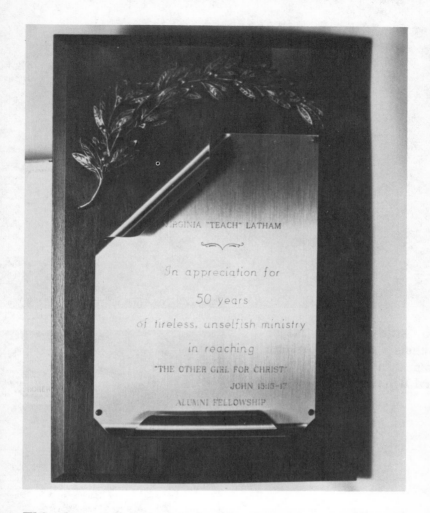

VIRGINIA "TEACH" LATHAM

In appreciation for

50 years

of tireless, unselfish ministry

in reaching

"THE OTHER GIRL FOR CHRIST"

JOHN 15:15-17

ALUMNI FELLOWSHIP

This plaque was presented to Teach at the conclusion of a surprise "This is Your Life" skit by alumni at Camp Awana.

Bible study is a major emphasis at an Awana Scholarship Camp for award-winning clubbers.

The awards worn by this Scholarship Camper show that she has completed all the achievements offered by her Guard Club.

This view is dear to the hearts of hundreds of campers at Camp Awana in Wisconsin.

Doc, wearing a chief's head-dress, enters into the spirit of a special event at Camp Awana.

In 1978, three sky divers landed in a pre-arranged area at Camp Awana, and Doc later posed in their gear. The bearded diver on Doc's left is Ken Rorheim, Art's son.

Scholarship campers proudly display the Timothy Awards they earned for three years of handbook achievement.

"A year later, my friend wrote me, saying that he was very sorry but he needed $1,000 of that loan immediately. It was visitors' day at our camp when I got the letter. Without her knowing anything about this, the mother of our youth director at that time said to me. 'Lance, I've got a burden on my heart that you need some money. Will $1,000 help?'

"This is only part of the story of God and His goodness and how He took care of all our needs. Our financial burden was especially heavy inasmuch as both the building of the camp and the construction of the Center church building came at about the same time. However, we were never embarrassed financially at any time."

One of the main concerns was that a new source of water would be found. The spring on which we were depending had been condemned and therefore a water driller *must* find water, for now only one day remained before the campers would arrive. We prayed and drove the pipe into the ground. Then, just like a miracle, there was water! Things were ready and just in time, for the buses arrived with a load of young people and another summer's program began.

Indeed, this was only part of the story. The marvelous account of Camp Awana can never be told merely with figures concerning finances and buildings. The story was and is essentially that of a growing tide of boys and girls, young people and their parents who, thirsting for reality, came to camp to hear the Word of God and study the Scriptures. It is the story of rows and rows of young people with shining eyes gathered about a camp fire and gaining impressions that would last forever. Some of these impressions were of Lance Latham, dressed like an old Indian chief, presiding over some initiation rites. Or demonstrating a stunt on the horizontal bar. Or riding a horse during mock ribbon-cutting ceremonies to open a new path. During one Bible message time, when the natives seemed more restless than usual, Doc sighed, "I seem to be casting pearls before swine today," and the campers settled down to pay attention. Others remember Teach saying on many camp occasions, "Girls, think of others!"

Lance and Virginia received citations in 1971 from Christian Camping, International, honoring them for 50 years of fruitful ministry in this challenging field. In 1978, Doc and Teach completed 57 years as camp directors. We know of no one else who has achieved such a record of continuous camping involvement.

Camp Awana is the story of waterfront activities where young athletes excelled in swimming and brought that same excellence to the life lived for Christ.

Camp Awana is the story of young people, motivated to live for the Savior, who returned to their homes, schools or churches to be witnesses for Christ as never before.

It is the story of boys and girls responding to an invitation to receive Christ and testifying within days that there never would be another day like this one.

Camp Awana is the story of thoughtful young Christians turning their backs on all that the world would have to offer and saying yes to the will of Christ and His call to the mission field, to the ministry, and to a lifetime of Christian service. That story continues today in Latin America, Africa, New Guinea, Europe, and the islands of the sea.

Out of the experiences at Camp Awana grew a mounting conviction on the part of the leadership that an association must be developed that could sustain and promote the lessons learned in youth leadership in a transmittable form so that they would be available to churches and youth groups across the nation and around the world. Indeed, it would be the story of the beginning of the Awana Youth Association.

Thousands of American young people will never forget their impressions at the testimony meetings at the last night of camp. They still would have tears in their eyes upon singing,

Camp Awana, camp for me,
And it's there I long to be.
Lakes and trees and skies so blue,
When I'm gone I'll dream of you.
When the sun goes down on the old campground,
Laughing voices happy and gay,
Camp Awana, camp for me,
And it's there I long to stay.

13

I Feel So Sorry for the People of the World

"You're drunk — it's time you went home!"

These words reminded the happy conventioneer that he was indeed drunk. The bars of Chicago's Rush Street and this last round at the nightclub had done him in. It was time to go home. He staggered out of the lighted doorway onto the sidewalk of North Rush Street. He made his way with an unsteady gait along the curb, hoping to hail a passing taxi. At just the right moment, he turned and saw a sign on what appeared to be a nightclub, causing him to exclaim, "Whaaht-iz-zat?" He was focusing his eyes on a sign on the nightclub doorway that said "New Tribes Mission."

From inside he heard the strains of a song just loud enough to arouse his curiosity. He eased over to the doorway and decided that perhaps it wasn't time to go home after all. He slipped into the back of the hall to listen. There stepped to the platform a speaker who began to deliver an electrifying message. He talked about sin and the judgment of God and the necessity of reaching a world for Christ. Before the evening was over, the conventioneer became a child of God. As a Christian, he established the direction of his life to go to reach a world for Christ. He had been captured by the message and the ministry of a man before whom no one could remain neutral.

The speaker was Paul Fleming.

Paul Fleming became the third Paul in the life of Lance Latham. Lance once confided to me in another moving moment of our conversations together, "Dave, there are three people who have influenced my life more than any others beside Jesus Christ Himself, and all of their names are Paul. I am referring to the Apostle Paul, Paul Rader and Paul Fleming."

It was back in the old Tab days that Paul Fleming came to Christ. Under the preaching of Paul Rader, he made a burning commitment with the whole of his life to serve Christ as a missionary. Paul Fleming became the founder and first director of New Tribes Mission.

Few preachers of the gospel ever moved an audience as did Paul Fleming. The result of listening to Fleming's forty-five-minute challenge to missions was a nearly physical impact on the minds and hearts of his hearers. He would preach with great intensity, many times heedless of the fact that his tie was slung over his left shoulder. With singleness of purpose, he would press the point that the world was dying "for want of what you people so richly enjoy here this evening, the privilege of knowing Jesus Christ and understanding the gospel."

Paul Fleming was convinced that the normal, healthy Christian who did not allow for the possibility that God wanted him on the mission field was outside the will of God. He echoed the message of Oswald J. Smith in Toronto, saying, "Why should anyone hear the gospel twice before everyone has heard it once?" The need of the world and the awful cry of heathenism was the pressing, consuming preoccupation of his life. Nothing mattered but mobilizing the largest number of people in the shortest amount of time to become a new army of spiritual conquest to the ends of the earth.

Paul Fleming shunned some of the popular concepts in missions. He argued that missionaries all too often went to the sheltered enclaves of big cities in foreign lands, there to sort out spiritual trappings that were no more effective there than in the church back home. He decried the tendency of missionaries to build for themselves circumstances of comfort even in faraway lands.

"The people who need to be reached with the gospel are those in darkest heathenism who have never once heard the name of Jesus Christ. They are the people in the tribes, and there are thousands and thousands of new tribes that are as yet untouched with the gospel." For Paul Fleming, world missions was not the common, ponderous approach of people who took years to prepare and even then were ineffective. For him, the burning heart was a greater consideration than the long-range plan.

Those were the years of World War II, and exploiting this analogy, Paul Fleming would say, "You may be 4F with Uncle Sam, but you're 1A with the Lord. He can use people with one leg, one eye, just so your heart is full and your position is straight."

Like a bulldozer moving through the straw huts of archaic ideas and unworkable plans, Paul Fleming cut a swath through the Christian community of Chicago, the Midwest, and in fact the United States that could not be ignored. Few could remain neutral to his presentation. Some reacted negatively to his fierce pragmatism and his single-minded message. Others in great numbers were inspired to a level of commitment to Christ which they never would have dreamed of. Forsaking what to them now were lesser plans and smaller goals, they gladly and sacrificially joined the cause of world missions under the leadership of Paul Fleming.

Paul landed like a bombshell in Chicago and at the

Lance and the man who became the "third Paul" in his life, Paul Fleming, stop for a moment before a board meeting of New Tribes Mission.

New Tribes missionaries on board the plane belonging to the mission are eager to arrive at their new assignments.

Center. His preaching of the challenge of world missions electrified the audience and also the pastor of the church — Lance Latham. Lance had received a great vision for world missions from the heartfelt call of Paul Rader. Paul Fleming now galvanized that world concern in Lance's life. From that moment on Lance was never the same. He would extend the imperative call for missions to everyone he met. Paul Fleming was Lance's man from Macedonia.

In Lance's own testimony, he says, "Paul Fleming came back from Malaya broken in health. He had many missionary years behind him, but especially three years in Malaya where he had contracted malaria. Many were the miles that he traversed in Malaya, the latter part of these with some of his converts, traveling in a station wagon. William Turnbull of the Christian and Missionary Alliance says that Paul must have won 3,000 souls to Christ in those three years. He finally had to give up missionary work and return home, uncertain whether he could ever do missionary work again. Here again, the encouragement of a wonderful man like Paul Rader had much to do with his restoration to health and ability to resume missionary work. The recommendations of a respected friend brought Paul Fleming to the Center — this was in the year 1942. He had the same fire and ambition that he had previously had."

The bond of love between Lance Latham and Paul Fleming was instant and permanent. "Doc, we must organize a new mission that will reach the heathen for Christ. Our existing missions have settled into organizational senility. They labor in the major cities, depend too much on education, and they are simply not doing the job. No one is really reaching the tribespeople of the world for Christ." Lance agreed and the decision was made to take a new and giant step of faith in the organization of a mission board which would reach into the darkness where others had not gone before.

Lance remembers, "I have always rejoiced at the first New Tribes committee meeting which was held at our camp in Michigan; our first Bible school for missionary volunteers, held at the Center; our first broadcast together with New Tribes; and likewise our first magazine, *The Life Line*.

"Paul Fleming lived one thing, thought one thing, dreamed one thing. I believe that down in his heart he felt that everyone should go to the mission field. The Center had been in operation for about eight years, and we had only four foreign missionaries. Paul Fleming's coming to us on subsequent visits awoke us from our sleep. One after another of our young folks were volunteering for the field. In fact, some enrolled in New Tribes and went to the field without even filing an application to the Center expressing the purpose in their lives.

"In practically every case, we began to sense what had happened and pledged these wonderful young folks regular support. Paul and the New Tribes Mission have never encouraged their missionaries to ask for support, but to obey God and believe Him that He will supply their need."

The first organizational meeting of the New Tribes Mission was held at Camp Michawana in 1942. Lance Latham was on the original board and from the first, was the treasurer of the mission. These young leaders knew little about the "proven methods" of missions which, in their minds, had been less than effective. Their solidarity and concern, however, centered around a burning heart; a heart that was first consumed with a love for Christ and a similar consuming passion for the heartbreak of a lost world. Lance Latham, in the ministry of New Tribes and Paul Fleming, found a vehicle that could be an instrument to world outreach consistent with the grand dynamic of his own life.

While yet a young man, Lance, in the hearing of his sister, said in a pensive moment, "I feel so sorry for all the people of the world, but I know that only Jesus Christ can help them." Now, in addition to his other labors, Lance Latham threw himself without reservation into the new challenge, New Tribes Mission.

The first contingent of missionary volunteers were eight in number. The first Bible school and training classes for them were held at the Center on Fullerton Avenue. Lance Latham was the teacher, instructing this first group of young evangels of the cross in the proper understanding of Scripture.

The proper understanding, of course, was the message of the gospel of the grace of God. The book was Romans, and it was taught with the conviction that no work for Christ could be effective unless it was built on "the message," the Pauline revelation of the grace of God.

"The message is the method," was Doc's conviction. All of his life he was unimpressed with methodology as it was taught in Christian educational institutions. His lifelong experience had produced the conviction that while methods were necessary, the message was the essential issue. For him, the person who believed the message of the gospel of the grace of God would produce results even if his methods were poor. Conversely, a person who was well-versed in methodology would nevertheless ultimately fail unless he had truth to believe. Methodology is like the pipeline, but the message of the gospel is the fresh water that is carried to its destination. So it was that New Tribes was initiated with the combination of the zeal of Paul Fleming and the Bible teaching of Lance Latham.

So also did it continue. Out of concern for the truth to be implanted in the lives of young missionaries, Lance gave himself to conducting Bible classes for them on a regular basis. Into his eighty-second year of life, Lance continued to travel weekly to the New Tribes headquarters in Woodworth, Wisconsin to conduct Bible classes for the missionaries. "Believing and knowing the truth will do them more good than anything else," he would continually insist.

New Tribes Mission began its existence with offices at 71 North Rush Street on the Gold Coast of Chicago, but worked very closely with Doc and the North Side Gospel Center. According to Kenneth Johnston, chairman of the New Tribes Mission, "The first periodical that we as a mission used in getting the message of the mission out to the public was graciously shared by the North Side Gospel Center and Doc Latham in what was then known as the *Life Line* magazine. This magazine was a real blessing and also proved to be so for the fledgling New Tribes Mission. Also, the first broadcasting that New Tribes Mission ever did was in cooperation with the North Side Gospel Center and their Life Line broadcast."

Johnston continues, "Doc Latham was one whom the founder of New Tribes Mission, Paul W. Fleming, chose to have with him and others on the first executive committee of New Tribes Mission. Along with Paul Fleming and Lance Latham were Merv Roselle, Cecil Dye who was later killed by Indians in Bolivia, Roy Oestreicher, Bill Dillon, and Bob Williams, who for many years has served on the field of Borneo in the South Pacific."

The early days of New Tribes Mission and the outreach of the North Side Gospel Center were not without threadbare moments and great difficulties. Johnston reports, "When our first sixteen men, women and children under the leadership of Cecil Dye, one of the executive committee members, were about to leave

Chicago for Bolivia, South America, Paul Fleming went to Doc and asked him if it would be possible to use the Center's bus, which was an old cross-country bus. They needed some sort of conveyance that would take all sixteen of these folks along with their baggage to the port of exit at New Orleans, Lousiana. Doc said that he was sure that the Center would be happy for the mission to use the bus, but assured them that the bus had been nothing but trouble. It never went anywhere without a flat tire or something or other going wrong with it. He said, 'If you want to take it with that understanding, you're welcome to.' Paul Fleming knew what the needs of the mission were and accepted the offer. The trip was made to New Orleans, taking all the folks and their baggage, and arrived back again in Chicago. Doc Latham asked how the bus had performed, and Paul Fleming said that they had not had a minute's problem with it from the time they left until they returned to Chicago. In recounting this situation, Doc has often said that the miracle of getting passports and visas during the war, plus God's sending in the finances for this whole party to go to Bolivia with all their necessary equipment, was no greater miracle than the miracle of the Center bus making this round trip without trouble!"

No program of spiritual conquest has ever been without its casualties, and it was in these early years that tragedy struck. The news at first was sketchy, and then it was confirmed as a great tragedy in the saga of world missions. Bolivian natives assaulted that first contingent of missionaries and again the blood of the martyrs became the seed of the church. Cecil Dye, Bob Dye, Dave Bacon, George Hosbach, and Eldon Hunter gave their lives for Christ in the jungles of Bolivia.

Sorrows come in sizes proportionate to our ability to bear them. God must have esteemed the young mission and its mentor greatly able to bear such sorrow, for soon tragedy struck again. On November 21, 1950, the plane taking off from California wheeled into the clouds enroute to South America. Within minutes, it was a sheet of flame on the side of a mountain. Besides the missionaries and crew, the founder of the mission, Paul Fleming, was aboard. The beating heart of this young pioneer had been stilled on earth as he was translated to heaven. Also aboard the plane were missionary Edna Grenur and her five children, Donna Wetherald and her son, and a number of others, whose names are in the Book of Life.

Paul Fleming and his short but eventful life will stand through all the annals of time as an example of sacrifice and selfless service for Christ. In the minds of many, his "can do" philosophy of Christian missions seemed too heedless of the problems, bordering on irresponsibility. Nothing could be further from the truth, but rather one must feel that a life lived with the velocity by which he lived would, under the best circumstances, not last for long. Those Christians who looked upon his service for Christ are convinced that in the providence of God, he was used as the catalyst, the dynamite, the explosive force to begin a ministry. No doubt, without such people, great works for Christ would not have existed. Paul Fleming knew how to make things happen, a quality which is imperative in every generation and without which any church will know only impotent dreams.

Great responsibilities fell on Lance Latham now, and stronger shoulders could not have been chosen. The work continued to grow, and Doc participated in many ways. He taught the Bible, ministered in the New Tribes boot camps, and traveled the world.

Ken Johnston recalls, "The first time Doc came into boot camp, I was there when he arrived at around midnight. Paul Fleming and his wife had driven him from Sacramento to the base of the mountain near where boot camp was located. It was raining very hard so they phoned over a little single-wire telephone system that we had, asking if someone could come down and help them get into camp. I sent Bob Vawter, who was my helper during those days. He knew the road and was able to drive it under any conditions. When he got to where the Flemings and Doc were waiting, he took Doc with him and the Flemings followed. Bob drove the road very fast and gave Doc a vivid description of the deep canyon below, as well as the little narrow, winding, single-lane road around the edge of this mountain. When Doc got into camp he was so apprehensive that he could hardly talk. He told me that I should get after that young man! During the meeting that followed, Paul Fleming had some fun in regard to the remarks he made pertaining to Doc, and I recall how Doc sat down at the piano to play, and the number he chose was 'Nobody Knows the Trouble I've Seen.' This brought billows of laughter from the candidate personnel who were sitting there, enjoying it all.

"Doc has taught in all our boot camps, which now number seven throughout the United States and Canada. He has taken a week at a time in such a teaching ministry over the years. This ministry has been a great blessing to the mission and those of us who make it up. His ministry has always been one of tremendous inspiration and encouragement. The founder of the mission, Paul Fleming, was most anxious that Doc not only serve on our executive committee but that he also, especially in those early days, serve as our 'watchdog' for the mission to keep it straight in doctrine and faithful in teaching the gospel of the grace of God. Over these years, there have been various influences that have arisen, but in and through all of these, Doc has been one of the great steadying factors."

Lance Latham also took a very personal part in the

outreach of the mission across the world. Johnston remembers, "Doc has made a number of trips to various mission fields of New Tribes Mission. On several occasions we have traveled together. This has always proven to be a great blessing to me personally, and I know that this has also been true of our personnel on these fields who have gathered together for their yearly field conferences. Doc's message was always encouraging and uplifting to the missionaries who came to hear him.

"I remember when Doc and I went to Paraguay and made our way far into the interior of the Gran Chaco to visit some of our missionaries. On one occasion, we wanted to go through some of the scrub jungle to visit an Indian village. Doc would have to ride a horse! He said that he had ridden only once before as a little boy, so this was a new experience to him. While the horse was being saddled, we outfitted Doc in a cowboy hat, leather chaps and a bandanna. Then he tried to mount his steed. This was the most gentle, patient, understanding horse I've ever seen. It seemed like Doc would never get up into the saddle. Still the horse very patiently stood there. Doc sure looked funny! As we traveled, our way was through a swamp that had much water in it. The horses were in water so deep they were almost swimming. We all had to lift our feet out of the stirrups to keep dry. Doc just felt like he had to keep his feet in the stirrups, so through the water his feet and legs went. He told me later that he was just a little bit apprehensive.

"On another occasion, we traveled in Brazil far out to Macauba on the Bananell Island along the Tocantins River. When we arrived we had to get into a little dugout canoe. The four of us paddled across this big swift river. At that time we had about one inch of free board on either side, and the canoe, which had no keel on it, was very tippy. Doc wouldn't sit down in the canoe,

Art and Doc prepare to enjoy a meal in a straw hut during a trip to the hot and humid jungles of Venezuela.

A smiling new Venezuelan Christian, happy in the Lord, prepares dinner for her family.

The life of Peter Deyneka, founder of Slavic Gospel
Association, was drastically changed by hearing and
believing the gospel of the grace of God.

but squatted, holding on for dear life. I looked back at him about halfway across the river. He had a grim look on his face. After the crossing was successfully made, he assured me that he didn't like those little 'pecan shells!' "

A better understanding of this incident will come when we remember that Lance always was very afraid of water. He could not swim at all and wanted no part in any aquatic pursuits. His apprehension about airplanes will also lend understanding to Johnston's further description. "On another occasion, Doc traveled with our east Brazil field chairman and me in a little four-seat aircraft, flying several hours over a vast expanse of jungle. We had chartered the airplane, and the Brazilian pilot did a good job. We had almost arrived home after a successful round trip. We could actually see our destination, the town of Goias, when we entered a storm front. The plane was tossed around by violent updrafts and down drafts. The pilot struggled to keep the plane from falling out of the sky. Doc was holding on for dear life. At that time, he remarked, 'My wife always told me not to fly in these little airplanes!' We landed safely and without incident and were grateful to the Lord for His care and keeping.

"On one trip, we were able to travel together to Iguacu Falls on the Parana River not too far from where Paraguay, Argentina and Brazil come together. This overnight trip was a most lovely occasion and Doc later said that it was one of the delightful days of his life to be able to have the privilege of spending it in such a beautiful spot. The scenery and the falls were absolutely breathtaking."

Before the association with New Tribes Mission, the Center had sent out four pioneer missionaries to foreign fields. Florence Almen went to Africa under Baptist Mid-Missions, and is still active there, although past retirement age. Walter and Mildred Warfield served in

Brazil under the same mission board. Elaine Mielke went to Mexico and later married Cameron Townsend, founder of Wycliffe Bible Translators.

Doc says that probably 70 young people from the North Side Gospel Center have volunteered and then gone to the mission field. Dr. Burt and Ruth Long have served in Central Africa under Sudan Interior Mission for many years, as have Ed and Alberta Dubisz. Gordon and Lena Bishop and Marilyn Morgan work with the same mission board.

Now serving under New Tribes Mission are George and Eleanor Antelo, Ron and Avis Bodin, Tom and Linda Christensen, Jack and Dorothy Connor, Steve and Pat Karum, Ken and Carol Learned, Lee and Irene Temples, and George and Esther Wesley.

Besides Elaine Townsend, Cal and Cornelia Hibbard, Ray and Esther Holmbo, Jonathan and Roseann Johnson, William and Grace Merrifield, Gil and Marian Prost, Clifford and Fay Spracklin, Phil and Lorraine Staalsen, and Dorothy Svendsen serve now with Wycliffe Bible Translators on many different fields. Arnold and Kathy Mayer work with Africa Inland Mission, and Rick and Sandi Bravine and Mary Jonas have also gone out from the Center to foreign mission work. Jack and Grace Frizen served under Far Eastern Gospel Crusades, and Jack is now general director of the Independent Foreign Missionary Association.

Doc and the Center have had a mutually rewarding association for many years with Peter Deyneka and the Slavic Gospel Association, with its more than 150 missionaries among the Slavic people. Lance has served on the board of the Slavic Gospel Association during most of the years of its existence, and was chairman of the board for five years.

The privilege of knowing Jesus Christ and understanding the gospel of the grace of God implies responsibility. Over the years this principle was restated in many ways in the ministry of Lance Latham and the North Side Gospel Center. Under Lance's preaching, no young person was allowed to come to the conclusion that the grace of God meant license or irresponsibility. Again and again, without letup, young people were reminded, "Ye know the grace of our Lord Jesus Christ, that though he was rich, yet for your sakes he became poor, that ye through his poverty might be rich." The very same path of sacrifice was earnestly and always presented to the listening young hearts that gathered in successive waves of incoming boys and girls. Behind the sparkling music, the fun, the athletic programs and the relaxed gospel services, there soon became apparent a serious purpose. The program was grounded on the bedrock conviction that the gospel of the grace of God was life's greatest responsibility. This was of course the responsibility to become a custodian of that grace, bearing it as a precious substance out into the lives of others.

14

Into a New Era

"The war is over, Virginia, and I believe that a new world of opportunity is going to be coming upon us. We must pray that God will expand our faith and help us to be equal to the great challenge that lies before us."

Lance and Virginia talked with great concern about the progress of the ministries that had developed under their leadership. Their work had been solidly established in the city of Chicago and now it was apparent that larger things were before them for reasons that could not be ignored.

The war was over and the post-war era was churning with a new sense of opportunity and responsibility. Several dozen of the boys from the Center had gone to war in that five-year holocaust that recast the world into a new mold. Mothers and dads had prayed, trusting the Lord to protect their sons through the brutal battles in Europe, Africa, the South Pacific, Asia, and in the many places where men were involved in mortal combat. As an encouragement to their faith, Lance Latham had preached many times on the marvelous power of believing prayer. "When you know Christ as personal Savior, and when people are praying for you, you are as safe on any battlefield as you are in your own home here in Chicago. Let's always pray for our boys and especially trust God to help them to be a great testimony for Christ."

In 1945, the record of answered prayer was in. The Center had only one gold star on its service flag. Frank Gianesin died in action in Italy. His commanding officer said, "Frank was the bravest man I ever knew. When a fellow soldier was asked to undertake a dangerous job, Frank always offered to take his place, saying, "He is not sure of his eternal future if he dies. I am." Frank knew and loved the Lord.

What's more, these men returned with new ideas, new enthusiasms, new reasons to believe that God could use them and their lives in a special way for Christ. The new voltage of their faith had an electrifying effect at the Center; in fact the Christian boys who returned from World War II made an unforgettable impact upon the Church across America. They returned to quickly form new Christian organizations and start new programs of evangelism, missions, Bible teaching, and spiritual outreach.

Lance and Virginia considered some of the other blessings of God which were shaping the future of their ministry. The attendance and enthusiasm at the Center had now grown beyond the capacity of the Fullerton Avenue location. And what's more, the lease ran out.

The Center therefore moved into a time that some have called "the wilderness years." To accommodate the growing crowds, the Masonic Temple on West Irving Park Road was leased for the Sunday meetings. The seating capacity was twice that of the furniture store location and soon even this was filled to capacity. Other buildings had to be rented to accommodate the boys' and girls' clubs which were now growing beyond all earlier predictions. The Guards, Pilots, and leaders of that day will not forget the West Mansfield Avenue building that was rented for the youth program. It was filled to capacity night after night and now, in addition, 150 to 200 college-age young people were attending the

Saturday night youth programs. Your present author became the director of the college-age program along with his responsibilities as a leader of one of the Pioneer boys' groups and editor of its weekly paper. Similarly, many young people, converted to Christ during their high school years, had now been brought into positions of leadership. One of the open secrets of the success of the youth work at North Side Gospel Center over the years has been the availability of trained leadership. Doc was many times asked the question, "Where do you get those bright young men and women who seem to be so able to teach the Bible, lead singing, organize recreation, and communicate so well with boys and girls?" Doc's answer was always the same. "It's very simple, we raise our own. Teach young people the Word of God and give them the chance to be involved in a no-nonsense youth program and they will develop potential beyond what you could ever suspect. What's more, if you don't turn them into leaders, you haven't really done your job."

It became apparent during the wilderness years that the only choice was to build a new North Side Gospel Center. The blessing of God made this an obvious fact.

After much earnest prayer, a set of lots was purchased in the 3800 block of North Central Avenue. It seemed an enormous undertaking but the enthusiasm of the people and their confidence in the faithfulness of God convinced everyone that it was the right and inevitable path to follow.

Those of us who were present at the ground-breaking ceremony shared the conviction of Lance and Virginia that a new era was indeed beginning at the Center. Again the neighborhood people looked on as the crowd sang hymns and prayed that God would bless in this new undertaking.

Even the financing was a new thing. Pastor Billy McCarrell of Cicero Bible Church had instituted a novel

173

Doc

Teach

The dedication of the North Side Gospel Center building on Central Avenue was a long-awaited occasion for the membership.

program in the suburb of Cicero. He said, "Why cannot the Lord's people finance their own construction? Why do many thousands of dollars in interest have to be paid that will finance taverns, roadhouses, and enterprises that tear down the gospel?" So now for the first time, the Center organized itself into a corporation for the purpose of raising non-interest-bearing loans for the construction of the new Center. People believed the Lord that this venture would succeed, saving potentially hundreds of thousands of dollars in interest payments.

At this point, something new occurred at the Center — membership. For fifteen years, the Center had carried on an amazing ministry without the actual existence of a membership roll. No one was a member, but enthusiasm was surely greater than among many of the members of the denominational churches of Chicago. The concept of church membership was therefore never a part of the basic approach to organization at the Center. You were either an enthusiastic participant or you weren't around. When speaking now about membership, Doc often quotes one of his younger followers, saying, "I realize that this idea of membership is new to you folks; in fact, as Dave Breese said, 'Why should I become a member? I am in it to the neck anyway.' Now Dave is six and one-half feet tall and so that means something. But the government has told us that we cannot legally accept the loans of our people unless we have actual membership rolls, so it has become a necessity in the building of our new church structure."

The years 1946-1949 brought the beautiful new building. It was built for approximately $300,000 on interest-free loans from hundreds of Chicagoans, some "members" of the Center, and others who saw the astonishing impact of its youth program and who wanted to have a part.

John Hansen, member of the Center, was construction superintendent. Much of the work was done with volunteer labor after the basic structure was up. It seemed that nothing could stand in the way of the growing tide of enthusiasm and confidence in the future which lived in the hearts of the people.

Lance and Virginia also viewed the fact that Camp Awana had now come into existence as another evidence of the blessing of God. By 1949, the property near Milwaukee had been purchased and many buildings erected. The summer camp program was therefore no longer at the mercy of state officials in various rented camps, but now the North Side Gospel Center owned its own camp. Camp Awana was a great evidence to all of us that God was surely bringing us into an era of wider opportunity.

A thousand young people every summer and 200 competent leaders were now gathering for the adventure that was Camp Awana. It was fast gaining a reputation as one of the most dynamic and spiritually profitable camping programs that was available to young people anywhere in America. Camp Awana pointed to a brilliant future.

The missionary program at the Center had also gathered remarkable force in the life of the church. The remembered enthusiasm of Paul Fleming and the present involvement with New Tribes Mission was a constant source of challenge to its young people. Dozens of them had responded to the invitation to invest their lives for Christ, bringing the gospel of the grace of God to the lost multitudes of earth.

The missionary force from the Center continued to grow, becoming a significant force in God's program of world missionary effort. There people stood at the center of a great responsibility for prayer and support, a central base of global outreach that took form in the lives of many.

A growing ministry in the future was also suggested by many other young people who had volunteered for the service of Christ in other ways. Pastors, Christian workers, evangelists, teachers were now moving into their beginnings of Christian service, having dedicated their lives to the service of Christ through the preaching of Lance Latham in these years at the Center. The commitment of these workers for Christ in America became living evidence of the glorious spiritual fruit which results from the preaching of the gospel of the grace of God.

Doc has always believed that a work for God must be unselfish in sharing its people, and that the real reason for the existence of a church is to gather in, win to Christ, train for service, and then send out. Art Rorheim remembers occasions when he had to watch his head leadership move away from the clubs at the Center. Jim Talbot wrestled with this before deciding to move his young family from Chicago to the suburbs, but he was instrumental in starting Awana Clubs there in Rolling Meadows. Jimmy Barker left a big hole in the Center club leadership when he moved on to serve God on the mission field in South America. Christian leaders are to rejoice as God allows them to have a part in influencing other believers before He decides to move them somewhere else on His harvest field.

"Best of all, Virginia, we can rejoice in that, at the Center, the message is still intact. Without compromise, we have stood for the inspiration of the Bible, the deity of Christ, the virgin birth, the premillennial return of the Lord, the hope of eternal life, and all of this based on the gospel of the grace of God. Liberalism still seems to be coming in everywhere, but we can thank God for the faithful folk whom God has given us who are spiritually competent and therefore, wherever they go, stand for the truth of the gospel." Indeed, this was and is the greatest asset of the ministry at the Center. Everyone knew that the Center was characterized by marvelous music, colorful youth programs and dynamic methods which were a perennial source of excitement to all who participated. Above all else, however, they knew that Lance Latham and all who were a part of the program at the Center could be counted on to take an uncompromising stand for the Word of God and the testimony of Jesus Christ. For Lance, nothing, not even death itself could ever change that.

Anyone who would understand the amazing success of this ministry must remember that first and above all else, the ministry of the Center was based on a message. That message, the faith once delivered to the saints, is the gospel of the grace of God. This is the truth of Scripture, the great Pauline emphasis on justification by faith alone. The result is now obvious, for the fruit of those years is apparent everywhere. The Center has never experienced a split and has been remarkably free from any form of spiritual defection. The testimony is clear that the preaching of the gospel of grace produces godly living, faithful service, and becomes a tremendous motivation for personal spiritual development. For the most part, the young people who committed their lives to Christ under the preaching of Lance Latham during those years were ordinary people who went out to perform many extraordinary tasks for the Lord.

The result is that, by the end of the 1940s, the ministry of Lance Latham had been developed under the leadership of the Holy Spirit into a force for spiritual conquest that was to become remarkable indeed. Quantity would now augment quality. Faithfulness would become fruitfulness in a way that would compare favorably to the ministry of significant leaders in any history of the Church of Jesus Christ.

15

The Spiritual Explosion

"Look, Doc, we need help. I was raised at the Center and now I am in Milwaukee as a youth director and I believe God wants us to do the same thing here."

"Dear Mr. Latham; Here in Pennsylvania we have heard about that amazing program which you have at the Center and how young people are coming to Christ by the dozens. Please send us a set of suggestions as to how we can do the same thing here in our city!"

Letters like this, and hundreds of others, began to arrive at North Side Gospel Center; 3859 North Central Avenue; Chicago, Illinois 60634. The inquiries which were coming in were probably inevitable. Independent churches, Baptist churches, Bible churches, in fact churches of many Protestant denominations were facing the near-impossible problem of setting up an effective youth program for their young people. Church boards discussed the subject of the future and increasingly realized that there is no future unless there is an effective ministry for boys and girls today. "But where are we going to get the leadership?" they asked. "Where do the materials come from? Who knows anything about the problem of interesting young people in the work of the church in this changing generation?" They asked these and many other questions and the answers seemed to be difficult, to say the least. In addition to Awana, emergent interdenominational programs have developed and experienced great success in hundreds of American cities. These include Youth For Christ, Child Evangelism Fellowship, Inter-Varsity Christian Fellowship, Young Life, High Crusader Clubs, Campus Crusade for Christ, and many others. There was no doubt that young people were looking for an answer, but the problem of an effective youth program seemed to be insufficiently answered in the churches.

The denominational youth programs appeared to be colorless and ineffective. Pallid Sunday School materials left young people without spiritual answers and hence without a continuing interest. The question therefore remained, "What is available to the church by way of an effective program for boys and girls, for young people, that can match the challenge of our times?"

The result was inevitable; letters poured into the North Side Gospel Center asking for help in setting up a program similar to the Awana activities that were producing such an effective answer on Chicago's north side.

Lance Latham gathered with the youth leadership at the Center to discuss the question. With him was the young genius who had already shown a remarkable ability in not only actually working with boys and girls, but organizing in an administrative sense the complicated structure of a church youth program. Art Rorheim was that man. His talent for youth organization had turned the biblical convictions and spiritual drive of Lance Latham into a marvelously effective program for boys and girls. Lance Latham knew what to believe, and Art Rorheim, who knew these things as well, also knew how to organize a program. The result was a spiritual explosion.

The discussion in 1950 centered around the best way to respond to the many inquiries which were coming in for programs like the one at the Center. When that circle of leaders prayed for those who were ministering for Christ in other places, they became convinced that God was laying upon them the responsibility to do something to help those others who were laboring for Christ in the larger circle of the Church. That conviction took concrete form. In 1950 the Awana Youth Association was organized.

Its first "office" took the form of a single desk and chair that found their place under a stairway in the basement of the Center. That office and a single typewriter were the beginning. The choice of a director for that budding organization also appeared to be inevitable — it was Art Rorheim.

Twenty years earlier, Art had been won for Christ through the ministry at the Tabernacle. Who could have known, when Art accepted Christ as his personal Savior, the ministry that God had in mind for this teenager who had come to Christ?

Lance Latham himself recalls his impressions of those days. "Art Rorheim was a member of our White Shirt Brigade and all of our Bible classes years before I began to realize that God had given us a great leader. He came to the Lord through the death of his brother Roy. I visited Roy in the hospital when he had spinal meningitis, just two or three days before he died. Art's father was also there. Art was standing at the door and heard Roy say to his father, 'And, Dad, don't forget to pray for Art. Art is not saved!' This wrenched Art's heart. Very shortly after, he believed on Christ as his Savior.

"The leader of the Pals at that time had slipped into worldliness. We did not know where to turn for a leader. Art was young but seemed to be the one best fitted. It was the same group of leaders under him, but the work began to grow. Two years later he added the Pioneers to his responsibility and some years afterwards, the high school boys. Among the three groups, we could just about count on 175 boys every Sunday in Sunday School. The week-night meetings were much larger.

"Both Art Rorheim and Truman Robertson asked to be put on the staff of the Center. 'We'll work for anything you'll give us, and we'll triple your boys' work.' The Center committee felt that we could put Art on the staff. Art and his wife had two small children. The Center was running close financially. I think Art earned about a third of what he was getting at a good war-time job. He did not mention money to me all of the thirty years he worked with me at the Center as our youth director. Truly he had the call of God in his heart.

"With this came the wonderful obtaining of Camp Awana, the success of which was more due to Art than we will ever know. Truly, the hand of the Lord has been upon Art Rorheim above everything we could ask or think.

"The same attitude in Truman Robertson is reflected in his wonderful North Woods Crusade, his all-year camp, and so much else." But of course, that is another story.

The early days after the formation of the Awana Youth Association were demanding indeed. It was soon recognized that some material needed to be printed that would explain the Awana program and help pastors and youth leaders to set up such a ministry in their churches. Down through the years at the Tabernacle and the Center, thousands of ideas, Bible lessons, projects and good approaches had been used at one time or another with great success. Now the problem was to bring these together into an organized approach which could be translated into other situations. It was obvious therefore that this would immediately demand writing, printing, leadership training, inspirational sessions, and of course, the money to pay for it all.

Art remembers some of the demands of those early days. "We were wondering how to get underway, for we hardly had a mimeograph machine. Then Victor Cory, president of Scripture Press and a longtime member of North Side Gospel Center, met with me. He was an expert on the production of Sunday School lessons and Christian literature and his help was invaluable. He pressed upon us the necessity of printing the first Awana manual and offered to pay for the typesetting and arrange for it to be printed at Scripture Press Publishers. Our friend Sketch Erickson, a former White Shirt Brigade member who at that time directed the art department at Scripture Press Publications, helped with our graphic arts format. We called the first manual 'The Hunter Handbook' and it was well accepted, leading to further requests. Vic Olson worked on layout and art work for the boys' handbooks, and Teach later adapted the books for girls, using her own illustrations and line drawings.

"We realized that we also must have a leaders' manual and so we worked hard to put this together.

"But of course, the problem was paying for it all. We got the idea of having big paper drives in order to raise the funds for the printing of these manuals. Week after week we had fifty kids and six trucks who would pick up papers in homes on Chicago's north side and then take them to the junk dealers to sell them. On a Saturday we would raise from $100 to $300. It was hard work but the money was needed and it kept us alive. It was impossible for us to appeal for funds because we had no mailing list and besides that, the needs of camp and the Center would take precedence in the minds of our friends above this unknown organization called Awana Youth Association.

"We soon built offices in the basement of the Center and began to work on displays, awards, and the other

The first Olympic Meets were held in the basement of the North Side Gospel Center.

material that was needed. We bought a printing press for $150 and, I assure you, we worked that printing press to death day and night to keep up with the requests that were coming in. Dan Mielke, a printer by trade, kept that press running and was able to procure other necessary equipment through his business connections. When Dan came to work with us full time, he directed the entire printing operation, operated the press, and supervised the kids who gathered after school to collate the printed material."

A young man by the name of Jimmy Barker helped develop the paper drives and worked every Saturday, faithfully calling boys, arranging for trucks and organizing the many details. Jim Barker also created most of the crafts that were used in Awana for many years. He worked out the entrance tests for the local Awana Clubs which are still in use in today's Awana program.

"Rich Wager was our first Awana employee," Art remembers. "He started working with me while he was still in Bible school, and later full time. Rich was my right arm, and I feel he is unequaled in creative club leadership. Besides playing a vital role in the early paper drives which paid our salaries, Rich spearheaded the printing of the first Awana handbook. He was the first editor of the *Signal* magazine, continues to write articles for us today, and has also written material for our Shipmate program. When Rich felt the Lord leading him in another direction, it was a great loss, but I knew God was speaking to him, and respected his decision. It is evident that it was the Lord's leading. Since then, he has organized a Christian day school at the church where he was youth pastor. In addition to pastoring Emmanuel Baptist Church in Berwyn, Illinois, Rich started two Christian camps, including Silver Birch Ranch in Wisconsin, which he directs today. Rich sponsored

Awana's first Scholarship Camp for award-winning clubbers, inviting us to use the facilities at Silver Birch Ranch."

Bill Merrifield added his bright young mind to the development of the materials and labored long hours to bring them into existence. By this time other churches wanted the material in increasing quantities because there was nothing else which had the biblical content, the organization, and the motivational factors contained in the Awana material.

A remarkable idea grew out of the early Awana scene in the form of the Awana Olympics. The first Olympic Meet was held in the basement of the Center in 1954. Today the Olympic program has grown to 100 meets across the United States, each with 16 teams of 17 members participating on four different game floor circles at the same time, rather like a three-ring circus. The ten Olympic games include races, relays, and balloon and bean bag events.

Another major factor in the growth of Awana was a new idea which occurred to the leaders at that time as well. Art remembers, "We were aware that boys and girls wanted to be identified with something that they could be proud of and even have some kind of an emblem of that identification. Consequently, we struck upon the idea of Awana uniforms. Our first uniforms were simply beanies. We got this idea because one of our friends found about a thousand of these small caps in an old trunk at the bottom of an elevator shaft in a building. My wife sewed emblems on all of these and our Awana clubbers began to wear them proudly. Then we began to use sweaters for all of our leaders, and these confirmed our idea of the value of a uniform. Now Awana produces a full uniform for boys and girls of every age. On their uniforms they wear emblems that tell the location of their Awana Club as well as the awards which they have received. We feel uniforms are a significant part of the Awana program."

Rorheim also became aware that, beyond the circle of churches in Chicago, the story of Awana needed to be told to those who had not had the chance to be a part of an Awana Club. He recalls, "The first display that we ever presented was at the National Sunday School Association convention in Grand Rapids, Michigan in 1954. We stapled pennants around the booth to add to its attractive appearance and had the chance to meet many new friends there. Despite our own impression of our growth, we realized that there were many who hadn't heard of Awana.

"This gave us the idea of doing a film. A friend, Bob Ford, also thought it would be possible, so he rented equipment and we produced a film called 'Hitting the Mark.' Jack O'Dell, who had been doing the scripts for Pacific Garden Mission's 'Unshackled' program wrote the script for the film and it really hit the mark for us. We made fifty or sixty copies of the film and it was shown in thousands of places across America, producing a new wave of interest in the Awana program."

The response was so great that it soon posed new expansion difficulties for Awana. Rorheim and the Awana staff were embarrassed at the need for more space, moving the printing operation into another one of the Center's basement rooms. Additional room was needed for supplies for the growing operation, so it became apparent that a new step must be taken. The basement at the Center could no longer contain the expanding Awana operations. By 1960, there were 900 Awana Clubs.

It is always true that where God leads, God supplies. Joseph Gunderson of Midwest Bible Church, a friend of the Awana program, located a building at 7511 West Belmont Avenue. So it was that in the winter of 1960,

Lance Latham and Art Rorheim labor together in the greatest mission field in the world, boys and girls.

Lance visits with his good friend Victor Cory, founder of Scripture Press. Victor was especially helpful in the early days of Awana.

Boys worked hard every Saturday collecting paper to support the growing Awana ministry.

Volunteers collated Awana materials in the Belmont Avenue Building.

Awana Missionaries are working for the Lord to expand and strengthen the Awana ministry.

Artist's drawing depicts the Awana Headquarters building in Rolling Meadows, Illinois.

Enthusiastic Sparks clubbers, boys and girls from kindergarten through second grade, listen eagerly to a Bible story.

This is a "total Awana family." Tim has earned his Meritorious Award, Carol her Timothy, Denise her Citation, and Debbie is an active Sparks clubber. Mr. and Mrs. Lester work closely with Awana Missionary Don Bunge.

Hundreds of spectators gather at a recent Olympic Meet to cheer for their favorite teams.

the small but growing Awana staff moved into the new facilities. "The new building seemed gigantic to us," remembers Art Rorheim, "but quickly our expanding volume of supplies, material and people began to fill the area."

Art also recalls, "When purchasing the new Belmont Avenue building, Awana needed to acquire a tax-exempt status. Attorney Jim Ferstel, of Catholic faith, was most competent in that area of law, and we retained him to represent Awana. It was interesting to hear him prove in court that Awana actually was a Christian organization, and he gave a clear-cut gospel presentation. As he quoted from the Awana constitution, he emphatically emphasized that the main purpose of Awana is to bring boys and girls to a knowledge of Christ as their personal Savior . "

By 1960, the growing number of Awana Clubs meant that multiple Olympic programs were being held. Always creative, the Awana leaders came up with a new idea of simultaneous Olympic contests being held in two circles at the same time before the crowd. Since then, the Awana Olympics has grown to four-circle meets, making it possible for teams from sixteen churches to participate in the same Olympic Meet. The simple idea of a four-circle Olympic program is indicative of the way the creative genius of Art Rorheim and his fellow-workers has been constantly applied to the new challenge of Awana development. Today there are hundreds of methods for doing things in the growing Awana program about which no book had ever been written. No Christian education program in any college or Bible institute at that time could ever have anticipated the needs of such a creative youth work or trained leaders in the Awana methodology.

During the years of 1958-1960, it became apparent that material alone could never tell the full Awana story in other cities. Too many questions had to be answered and too many things explained. The Awana board then met to earnestly pray that God in His wisdom would give Awana the people who could tell the story. Awana must virtually set up a "missionary program" to bring the word about Awana to those who were interested in producing such a program. About this time a gentleman from Omaha, Nebraska came to Art and said, "Is it possible that Awana would want a missionary to help organize Awana programs in other places?" The answer was yes, and so began the Awana Missionary program, with Don Bunge as the first missionary. The Awana Missionary program has now grown to include twenty-four missionaries in the United States, Australia and in Canada.

Even before Don Bunge joined Awana as the first full-time missionary, a Christian layman named Leo Spencer had been introduced to the Awana ministry. Clarence Jones, the first youth leader appointed by Paul Rader at the old Tabernacle and author of the Awana theme song, showed the film "Hitting the Mark" at the Arrowhead Camp in Pennsylvania. Leo obeyed the call of God and has been representing Awana on the east coast for twenty years. Now in the fall of 1978, his son Dennis is following in his father's footsteps as an Awana missionary candidate.

Because camping is an important part of the Awana program, many camps are now operating under leadership trained by and guidelines set up by the original Awana camps. In addition to these camping programs, five Scholarship Camps lasting one week each were conducted in 1978 across the United States for Awana clubbers who had earned their Timothy and Meritorious awards, the cream-of-the-crop clubbers.

So Awana continued to grow.

The decade from 1960 to 1970 continued that irrepressible program of expansion. By 1970, nearly 500 churches had joined the Awana program and 2,000 Awana Clubs were operating. The Belmont Avenue headquarters began to burst at the seams. Dan Mielke, converted to Christ at the old Center on Fullerton Avenue and expert printer, became the full-time printer for Awana. Out on the field, missionaries were added in Wisconsin, Michigan, and the eastern states, and the business obligations of Awana seemed to again approach the point where the existing facility could not contain them. Books were being ordered in huge quantities and materials of many kinds needed to be purchased in ever increasing quantities.

Winnie Rorheim was no small part of this. In a marvelous way, God gave to Art Rorheim a wife who put in the same kind of hours and committed herself to the same level of sacrifice as did her husband. Art and Winnie Rorheim were married by Lance Latham in the days of the old Center on Fullerton Avenue in the year 1939. Through the 1960s, Winnie still sewed emblems on neckerchieves and did the nameless, myriad things that no one ever hears about but which added that extra "certain something" to everything that Awana did. Beyond all this, she prayed for her husband and trusted that God would give them wisdom to keep up with the mounting tide of response that seemed to come from everywhere.

"At about this time," Art remembers, "the sheer volume of neckerchieves we needed began to overwhelm Winnie and her helpers, and I turned to the yellow pages of the phone book for help. Although we placed an order so small that it was probably a nuisance, the gentleman I talked with was friendly as he agreed to help us out. A year later when our uniform supply order fell through at the last minute, I remembered that kind man and asked him to recommend a uniform supplier for us. He suggested Joe Altfeld, and our association with Joe has been an unusually rewarding one. When other suppliers were not interested in a group as small as Awana, Joe Altfeld trusted us and invested over $100,000 in inventory so that he could supply uniforms as we needed them. It was another of the Lord's provisions at a time when we were wondering where to turn."

"Teach" was also involved to the hilt in all of these developments. The progressively larger and more colorful manuals all bore the imprint of Teach's artwork and spiritual influence. The early Awana books were largely a combination of Doc's doctrinal writings, Teach's artwork, and Art Rorheim's putting together the mechanics. In all of this, Lance worked to raise the funds. "Doc went to bat for us many times at the Center," Art remembers, "and tirelessly told the story across Chicago and other places so that people would help us meet the rising tide of response and the demands for money that it took in order to meet the opportunities that we were facing." Teach was responsible for the growth of the girls' portion of Awana, putting into print and club organization the lessons learned over the years of development since the old Tab days.

By 1970, the Belmont Avenue property seemed impossibly small. Warehouses were being rented in other places and something had to be done to keep up with the expanding program. Awana needed a headquarters building many times the size of the Belmont Avenue property. "Where shall we go?" was the question the staff faced.

Once again these were critical days of development and the Awana board gave itself to prayer. "I'll never forget that time," Art recalls. "Some property in Bensenville was offered to us but things did not work out and we couldn't complete the arrangements. Then we heard of a 1.6 acre tract in Rolling Meadows which might make a good location for the new Awana headquarters. When I first saw the property, it was flooded and I thought that this would never work. We took boring tests, however, and all was well. We purchased the property for $44,000, which we received in interest-free loans. Today this property is valued at more than eight times the original cost. People rallied to the cause. Our general contractor Henry Staalsen and his associate Chuck McWhirter really gave of themselves for the project. Henry was Doc's right hand man in the construction of the North Side Gospel Center and at Camp Awana, and put his whole heart into the work of the Lord. He continues to serve on the Awana Board of Directors today. The Brooks Excavating Company did the excavation, contributed fill material to raise the grade by 10 feet, and did the finished grading, all free, as a gift to the Lord.

"The story of the construction of the new building is another one of those miracle accounts of the working of the Lord. Jack Skaathun constructed the large foundation for the more than 12,000-square-foot building, having agreed to do this for $5,000 under the lowest bid received. Jack was saved at Camp Awana, and was concerned with us for the Lord's work. When the foundation was complete, Jack's mother said, 'Are you really going to send them a bill?' Jack contributed the entire job."

This story — a boy saved through the Awana program who later became a major part of its growth — could be repeated a hundred times. Jack Skaathun, as a lad in Chicago, was met by Art Rorheim on the street and invited to an Awana club. The result was that Jack became a Christian and went on to live for the Lord. "That is the split-second timing that only the Lord can do."

A young man with a religious background had been saved at Awana Club. He drove past Awana Headquarters on Belmont Avenue and saw the sign. He got out of his truck, came in to see Art and offered to do all the decorating in the offices in the new Awana headquarters. So Ken Pearson, painter and contractor, had his part.

Don Wubs, saved at the North Side Gospel Center, said, "Art, let me handle all the moving process from Belmont Avenue to the new headquarters." He lined up 40 volunteers with 10 trucks, a much better option than the $4,000 estimate received from a moving company. The Rand McNally Company contributed extensive new shelving just in time — two weeks prior to moving.

The architect of the new building was Wally Carlson, an Awana leader at Midwest Bible Church. Henry Staalsen, builder from North Side Gospel Center who was saved under the ministry of Paul Rader in the old Tabernacle days, built the building.

This amazing time of transition — which seemed to be the constant process at Awana in all of its history — is remembered by Art Rorheim. "Every step which we took was a new step. There was no precedent and we had no idea as to just how to do it. Therefore, the Lord had to help us, and He did. He sent in His people, one after the other at just the right time. We had no experience in the things that we had to do. Our job was to reach boys and girls for Christ, but we had to have the people who knew all of these other things that could make it happen."

By 1975, the 12,000-square-foot building was filled to capacity and a new addition was needed. Therefore, in 1975 a new construction program was initiated that expanded the existing building by three times. By this year there were 4,000 Awana Clubs and all of the related services had to expand to meet the challenge. In addition, 20,000 leaders needed training, inspiration, doctrinal orientation and help in running their clubs. The Awana "Signal," the small, bi-monthly magazine printed to keep up with the need for leadership inspiration, now was being mailed in quantities of 28,000.

By 1978, the Awana program numbered more than 7,000 clubs in 2,000 churches in the United States. Neckerchieves, shirts, blouses, T-shirts, awards, emblems, training manuals — thousands of items — all of these now needed to be bought by the carload and reordered again and again just to stay equal to the mounting demand.

From across the world requests began to come. Burt and Ruth Long, missionaries from the Center, organized Awana in Central Africa. Ed Reeves brought the Awana story to Latin America. A visit from Art Rorheim in 1977 encouraged new elements of interest in the Scandinavian countries. Requests came in from Brazil, the Philippines, and several European countries. In overseas situations, the Awana uniform takes a somewhat unique form. In New Guinea, clubbers simply wear a colored string around their necks, but the enthusiasm is just as great.

The statistics of these developments could fill many pages. Statistics alone, however, do not tell the story. Art Rorheim often remembers, "The Awana method is really a message, the gospel of the grace of God. The things we see happening result from the preaching of the truth of Scripture. The Bible is our only guidebook. Sometimes pastors would like to use Awana material if we would allow them to make some 'minor' doctrinal changes, but we are committed to the truth of the gospel of grace as God has revealed it to us in His Word."

This is certainly evident to any visitor at Awana Headquarters. One morning each week the entire staff of more than 60 people gather for something more than just an ordinary "chapel service." When I visited the headquarters recently, the staff was in the process of memorizing the book of Philippians and they recited the second chapter together. Every Awana employee is constantly motivated to learn the Word and to pray daily for Awana clubbers.

Many years ago Paul Rader said to Lance Latham, "Lance, when you work with young people, give them something real. Teach them the Bible and be sure that they know it thoroughly. When you take them to camp, don't just sit on a hillside and give them little meditations. Give them a solid hour of intensive Bible study, because if you don't, your program will be worthless. Whatever else you do for young people, be sure that the Bible is studied, memorized and takes thorough root in their lives." Lance Latham never forgot that short speech. The fact that he was named "Pastor of the Year" at the Sixth Annual Pastors' Conference at Moody Bible Institute in May, 1978, is proof of this. The ministry of the Awana Youth Association is living evidence that the Bible is not only the truth of God, but that it alone bears fruit in the producing of a successful ministry for Christ.

The Awana program today centers around weekday meetings for boys and girls from kindergarten through high school, reaching young people for Christ and then training them to serve Him. "Pals" is a club for boys from 3rd through 5th grade, and "Chums" is for the same age girls. "Pioneers" are 6th-8th grade boys; "Guards" are 6th-8th grade girls; and "Shipmates" is a coed high school club. A typical evening includes an active game time, a session for handbook achievement, and a devotional message. Besides the annual Olympic competition between local clubs, Awana is now developing a program of Bible Quizzing.

The newest program at Awana is "Sparks," originated in 1977. In response to many demands, Sparks was organized for children from kindergarten through second grade. Introduced at the Awana banquet in 1976, Sparks "took off" with such an instant response that it was almost mind boggling. Within a matter of a few weeks, eighty Sparks clubs were organized as grateful parents sent their small children to these excellent programs. Nora Whiteside, in the providence of God, became available to write and direct this program, and its present development borders on the amazing.

Scholarship camps are now conducted each year in which only young people who have received their Timothy or Meritorious Awards may attend. Here, bright boys and girls who have excelled in scholarship and Bible study gather for a week of the most stimulating youth camping known in Christian work today.

The Shipmate program was developed in the mid-seventies for senior high young people, again producing a remarkable response. An "All-Shipmate Scholarship Camp" was held in 1978 and was the object of the intense participation of these high quality young people.

In 1978, twenty-four Awana Missionaries are living with their families on their home mission fields, starting new Awana Clubs and strengthening existing ones. Two of these men and their wives grew up in the youth clubs at the North Side Gospel Center; Dale and Margo Howard and Arne and Charlene Abrahamsen. Sam Eisenback's wife Joyce came from the Center also, and these all are living proof of the axiom...if you want effective leadership, raise your own.

On and on the story goes. The gospel of the grace of God firmly implanted in young lives and motivating them to serve Christ produces results.

16

A Challenge and a Charge

"Who really is the man behind such a ministry?"

In my judgment, no biography is complete which does not give the reader an opportunity to see into the heart of the person about whom the author is writing. The most blessed spiritual association of my life has been the marvelous years in which I have had the opportunity to know Lance and Virginia Latham. Beginning with that April day in 1943 when I came to Christ under the teaching of Mrs. Latham, I have counted my opportunity in knowing these precious people as one of the greatest human gifts I have received from the Lord. Rich is the individual who in an entire lifetime has had the privilege of knowing two people of the quality and spiritual caliber of Doc and Teach. For this reason alone, my life has been rich indeed.

I therefore covet for every reader something of that same opportunity. My purpose in this labor of love has been the hope of putting into readable form a set of insights into the heart and life of Lance and his lovely Virginia. I am sure that the best way this can be done is to give you the opportunity to hear personally from them. I am happy, therefore, that it was possible for me to press upon them the task of summarizing in a brief form their hopes for those who, with younger feet and younger hearts, walk the path of life in today's world.

From Lance

It was my great privilege to work for fifteen years under Paul Rader, regarded by so many of us as the most effective preacher since D. L. Moody. Dr. James Gray, then the dean of Moody Bible Institute, called Paul Rader the greatest persuader the Lord had. We had glorious years under his leadership and ministry.

I remember when Mr. Rader put me in charge of youth work and the summer camp for boys and girls. That great leader valued his youth work. When Paul Rader purchased the land which today is known as "Maranatha," the first thing he did was to build two buildings for the summer youth camp, which we called "Chic-Go-Tab."

I valued the time he spent with me concerning the way camp should be run. One piece of advice he gave me was, "Lance, when you work with young people, give them something real. Teach them the Bible and be sure that they know it thoroughly. When you take them to camp, don't just sit on a hillside and give them little meditations. Give them a solid hour of intensive Bible study, because if you don't, your program will be worthless. Whatever else you do for young people, be sure that the Bible is studied, memorized, and takes thorough root in their hearts and lives."

This was somewhat different from my thinking at that time. I valued the Word of God, but thought, "Mr. Rader does not know boys and girls." But then I called to mind the 5,000 people coming each Sunday evening to the Tabernacle, the souls saved each night, the twelve-hour radio program every Sunday, and so much more. I then began to suspect that in all probability he knew a lot more about boys and girls than I ever could.

His advice was good and I determined to follow it to the letter. I recruited sixty boys and offered them a six-week camp on one condition — we would have three hours of planned Bible study every morning besides our meeting in the evening. The boys could pay to camp whatever they were able. I used the offerings of the White Shirt Brigade singing group to augment the camp expenses.

A verse which has greatly influenced our ministry to both older and young folks is Colossians 1:28, "Whom (Christ) we preach, warning *every* man, and teaching *every* man in all wisdom; that we may present *every* man perfect in Christ Jesus." *Every* man and woman, *every* boy or girl who is truly saved has *every* possibility to be a "workman that needeth not to be ashamed, rightly dividing the word of truth." There are *no* exceptions.

My dear friend Dave Breese, who has been so used of God in an ever-increasing public ministry and in his publications, has asked me to write what I think are the necessary ingredients to a fruitful ministry among boys and girls.

Realize Who God Is

I would seek to make them sure about their relationship to God through the Lord Jesus Christ and His work on Calvary. Help them understand who God is, that He is holy, that He can not overlook our sin. His holiness demands full payment for sin; He made this full payment by giving His Son to bear the sins of the world on the cross of Calvary. To be saved, we cannot offer God anything. We simply look to what He has done on Calvary and put our hope there. "To him that worketh not, but believeth on Him that justifieth the ungodly, his faith is counted for righteousness" (Romans 4:5).

Know God's Way of Salvation

I would stress the matter of presenting God's way of

207

salvation over and over until, as far as humanly possible, the boy or girl is on the right ground for salvation.

The young person should also understand why certain presentations of the gospel are misleading. He does not give his heart to Christ, give his life to Christ, surrender all, ask for mercy, or ask Jesus into his heart. He must listen to what God has done on Calvary and believe it was for him. Salvation is not what we do for God. Salvation is what God has done for us. The price for sin has been fully paid by the shedding of the blood of the Son of God. "Without shedding of blood, there is no remission of sins."

There is one system of presenting the gospel which makes much of four steps to be taken in order to be saved. We would agree with the first three steps. The last declares that believing in Christ is turning the direction of your life over to Him. I absolutely disagree with this. Believing in Christ is beholding Him in faith on the cross of Calvary. Again, salvation is not our work, it is His work for us.

Begin Teaching Doctrine Early

I know that some people will say that such doctrine is too deep for boys and girls. Paul Rader had an educator visit the Tabernacle, offering her the opportunity to survey our boys' work and give her opinion of the way we worked with the boys. Her report was something like this, "Well, you certainly do a lot of things wrong. I observed a boy sixteen years old teaching some twelve-year-old boys. He was actually teaching them doctrine. At their age, they should be told stories. And yet," she mused, "the boys were giving perfect attention and seemed interested. That I couldn't understand."

The sad truth is this — unless boys and girls are taught doctrine at an early age, they will never learn what truth is. That is why it is impossible to spend too much time teaching young folks the basic truths of the Bible. If the foundation is well laid, the work will abide. Both Art Rorheim and I believe in encouraging saved boys and girls as young as fifteen years old to hold classes and teach younger folks the Word of God. Again, if they do not begin early to give out God's Word, the chances are that they never will.

Memorize Hymns

Boys and girls should be encouraged to learn and sing hymns. I would have them memorize such well-known old hymns as "At the Cross," "When I Survey the Wondrous Cross," "Am I a Soldier of the Cross," "At Calvary," "Amazing Grace," and then some of the newer hymns such as "Heaven Came Down," "Jesus Is Coming," "Now I Belong to Jesus."

"Speaking to yourselves in psalms, hymns and spiritual songs, singing and making melody in your heart" is such a vital part in the growth of young believers. We do not include in this recommendation most of the modern folk song-hymns which have very little spiritual truth and are consequently of no value. Some will argue, "But the young folks love these songs." We are responsible to train them another way than in the ways of the world. They are not our leaders; we are their leaders. Years of camping with boys and girls have proved to us that leaders who love the Lord and His Word can see, as a result of faithfulness in these matters, boys and girls who love the Lord and love the hymns that have real content.

Read the Bible

Adult leaders should urge boys and girls to read passages of the Bible which speak of the greatness of our Lord, such as Isaiah 40, and the miracles in the Gospels. Study the great passages that relate to His crucifixion and death; wonderful Isaiah 53, Psalms 23 and 69. We are so apt, even though we know well the way of salvation, to forget who He was and is. We should have classes teaching the fundamental truths of the Bible. We should exalt before them many passages which declare that Jesus is God, that the Holy Spirit is God. It should be well established in their minds, with Scripture references, that the Bible is God's Word. To declare that the Bible merely contains the Word of God is as bad as unbelief. They should know the references and establish this truth.

Other Bible passages suggested for young Christians wanting to begin a regular Bible-reading program are: Genesis 22:1-14, Genesis 41, Exodus 2:1-10, Exodus 14, Joshua 6, I Samuel 17, I Kings 17 and 18, II Kings 4 and 5, Daniel 1-6, Matthew 21:1-17, Matthew 26, Mark 2:1-12, Mark 5:1-20, Mark 8:1-9, and the Book of Acts.

Meet for Bible Study

In addition to regular, individual Bible reading, each person should be encouraged to meet with a group for Bible study. The issues are so tremendous. The future of everyone is either eternity in hell or eternity in heaven. Attending a good Bible class will help young people to become aware of the issues of life. Then, they will learn God's solutions to man's problems. A good Bible class is not a discussion group where "smatterings of ignorance" are shared, but rather one in which basic truths of the Bible are studied in depth. The most helpful Bible class is one which seeks to win others to Christ.

There are other vital elements necessary for a fruitful Christian life. First, we would encourage young people to find a Bible-believing church, a church with activities for young folks, a church where the truth of grace and our eternal security in Christ is preached. Second, young people should find a boy or girl their own age with whom they feel at home, so that they can read their Bibles and pray together. Third, they should try to visit other boys and girls who don't know the Lord and lead them to Christ.

Let's Work God's Way

When ministering to boys and girls, it is important for us to work God's way. We will notice in Paul's Epistles, and I am thinking especially of Romans, Galatians, Ephesians and Colossians, that the Apostle Paul does not immediately exhort and correct and challenge. He first lets us know what we have in Christ; God's purpose for us not only now, but through eternity.

The great climax of the Apostle Paul's prayer in the third chapter of Ephesians was that we "might be filled with all the fullness of God." But what is the path into this fullness? We do not obtain this fullness through yielding, or confessing our sins, as is so often taught. Paul is praying that God would give them "according to the riches of his glory, to be strengthened with might by his Spirit in the inner man; that Christ may dwell in your hearts by faith; that ye, being rooted and grounded in love, may be able to comprehend with all saints what is the breadth, and length, and depth, and height, and to know the love of Christ, which passeth knowledge, that ye might be filled with all the fullness of God." The revelation of God's love is His entrance for you into His fullness. This is a far better foundation than our changing attitudes, no matter how sincere we may be.

The Apostle Paul puts this and like revelations before his exhortations to us. Let's work God's way with the young folks. He put wonderful Romans 5-8, and especially Romans 8:18-39, before Romans 12:1. He puts Ephesians 1-3 before Ephesians 4 and 5. He puts Colossians 1 and 2 before Colossians 3 and 4. We are wise to work God's way. We are reminded of the wonderful things God has provided for us in Christ *before* we are exhorted to godly living.

Discover God's Infinite Love

We cannot begin too early to declare to young folks these glorious facts about their relationship to Christ, what He thinks of them, what He has planned for them. We are too apt to heap responsibilities upon them, even to make their service to Him a legal obligation, rather than a labor of love. We must remember, "Though I bestow all my goods to feed the poor, and though I give my body to be burned, and have not love, it profiteth me nothing."

A little nine-year-old boy approached me at Camp Awana one day. He was only the third person in my 84 years, and 63 years as a Christian, to ask me if I was saved. I assured him that I was. He then ventured, "Doc, I was saved a week ago last Monday. My, it's wonderful to be saved. And to think that I'm going to walk the golden streets. And I'm going to see Jesus face to face. I can hardly wait to see Him." He had the right idea. This affair with God and His Son is a love affair. People need to know about God's great love for them. The great burden of Paul Rader's sermons on Sunday mornings was to persuade Christians that God loves them.

It is never too soon to begin teaching boys and girls some of the amazing truths about God's love and plan for them. They are not creatures by an accident, unplanned, but rather "created in him from the foundation of the world, that we should be holy and without blame before him." They are to be "to the praise of his glory." They are to be His exhibits before "the principalities and powers in heavenly places." "That in the ages to come he might show the exceeding riches of his grace and his kindness toward us through Christ Jesus." They are to have a body like His glorious body. They are to be like Him.

Living in these glorious truths is to recognize that they are not under law but under grace; deserving nothing, but possessing all things.

Begin Life's Greatest Adventure

I'd like to impress upon young folks when they have been saved that they are entering life's greatest adventure. Nothing that earth can offer, no position, no financial allurement, can begin to compare with the opportunities God offers...and also the responsibilities. The rewards will be those which all the money on earth cannot buy. Young Christians have the opportunity of winning other boys and girls to Christ, and one soul is worth more than the whole world. God has delivered us from the power of darkness and has translated us into the kingdom of His dear Son. We have the most powerful weapon, the gospel of Christ, which can change eternal destiny. "He died for all, that they which live should not henceforth live unto themselves, but unto him which died for them." They are immediately His ambassadors, a greater job than being an ambassador to any foreign country.

Be Successful

Sometimes we see activities or accomplishments in the lives of boys and girls which we equate with success. Not that I would belittle Scripture memory contests, points and rewards. However, unless the time arrives in the life of the young person that he values the Word of God, that he lives the Word of God, and has a real desire to know that Word, we have not reached our goal as Bible teachers and youth workers.

My father taught me two verses a day from when I was four until I was fourteen, and this with plenty of reviews. I recited at one sitting the books of Romans,

John and James when I was seven years old. In all of those years, and even until I was twenty-one years of age, I never opened the Bible to read because I wanted to. This doesn't mean that I regret having learned all of those verses, nor underrate the faithfulness of my father in seeing to it that I learned them.

However, all those early years I appeared to others to be especially successful in two areas. First, some may have thought I was a fine pianist; perhaps outwardly I was. But inwardly I had no goals, no ambition. I had been *taught* the mechanics of piano, but had not *caught* the passion, the consuming desire for it. Not until an encouraging word fanned an inward flame did I begin to experience real success as a pianist.

Second, some may have thought I was a successful Christian because I had memorized vast quantities of Scripture from an early age. Outwardly, I perhaps appeared successful. But inwardly I was not saved. Again, I had been *taught* the mechanics — this time Scripture memory — but had never *realized* my need for salvation. From September 18, 1915, the Bible was a new book to me. Many were the times that I spent the whole morning with the Bible and a hymnbook, and was thrilled as I read the Bible and sang the hymns.

Filling the mind with Scripture is good, but only a means to a greater goal. It's when the heart responds to the Scripture, to the moving of the Holy Spirit, that boys and girls are born again and begin to love the Word of God.

We begin to be successful with our young folks when the hours of teaching the Bible beget a love for the Bible and stir up in their hearts a real desire to read it and delight in it.

From Virginia

Doc has been a wonderful husband. We kept company for two years and we delighted in being in the

214

Lord's service. We read the Bible together and talked of spiritual things constantly. He really took time to get me straightened out in what it means to *live* under grace as well as to be *saved* by grace. He was a godly boy with high standards and that is what I wanted. Not any old fellow could get my attention and all of this was because I really wanted God's will more than anything else. It must be very difficult for a Christian girl to be married to a carnal Christian who has no real interest in God's program for him.

Every summer since 1924, with no exception, we have gone to camp separately. We belonged to the Lord before we belonged to each other and so it has been in all we have done through the years — the clubs, camps, Bible classes, and the many duties of the North Side Gospel Center. When the clubs grew into an organization to meet the requests of many for our materials and ideas, the work was difficult but very precious, as a few of us (Art Rorheim, Rich Wager, Dan Mielke, Lance and I) worked on the books, badges and construction of Awana Clubs. What a rewarding ministry it has become to hundreds who work in Awana Clubs today.

Dave Breese has asked that I add a few words of counsel.

1. Be sure that your salvation is based on the *finished work of Calvary* alone with no additions of works or rituals. The shed blood of Christ was a complete price paid to guarantee heaven for you. The Holy Spirit will enter your life automatically when you do this and He will be the perfecter, as you grow in the Lord.

2. Next in importance is God's Word — not service. *Study your Bible.* Get into it thoroughly. II Timothy 2:15 became the verse on which our clubs were based. It is your tool for *effective* service. It is the only spiritual food on which you can become strong in the Lord. The Holy

Spirit within you will then begin to operate in your life, for it is *His* work to guide you into all truth and turn the light on Christ, whom He magnifies. Fall in love with Jesus and His love will constrain you into service.

3. Be careful in choosing your church and friends. Both can either help or ruin you. Be sure you are hearing the gospel of grace in the church you attend and be sure all of your real friends are saved and have the same spiritual goals that you have. If they "love the world," drop them as your companions. None of us live to ourselves. We rub off on others and they on us.

4. Pray about your important step in romance and marriage. Nothing can be more ruinous to a Christian boy or girl than to marry the wrong one. If your life is separated unto your Savior who died for you, you will be looking for that same kind of mate and the two of you can walk together in agreement on spiritual values and standards.

5. Don't drift from one thing to another. Find God's job for you and stick with it and be a workman "that needs not to be ashamed" of the results of your labors.

My verse for you all — "that in ALL things HE might have the preeminence" (Colossians 1:18).

And so I give you Lance and Virginia Latham, whose lives are for me a testament of grace.

Lance and Virginia Latham, with author Dave Breese